HOW DESIGNERS THINK

HOW DESIGNERS THINK

Bryan Lawson

The Architectural Press Ltd: London

First published in 1980 by
The Architectural Press Ltd: London

Paperback edition 1983
Reprinted 1986

© Bryan Lawson 1980

ISBN 0 85139 852 9

Printed in Great Britain by
Mackays of Chatham Ltd

Contents

Author's preface

This book draws on the research work of design methodologists and experimental psychologists over the last two decades. It forms an introduction to the skills of the designer which is intended for students in the early years of courses in architecture, planning, industrial and interior design. It is not so much a methodological instruction manual but more an outline of the many and varied mental tasks involved in the process of designing. Thus the student is introduced to the range of situations that he must learn to master, but is left to develop his own unique combination of techniques and strategies.

Various kinds of thinking are described and their respective advantages and limitations compared. The reader is recommended to practise and develop the breadth and depth of his thinking skills. The nature of design problems is explored, and some routes through them are mapped out. Mental techniques for use at key points along these routes are described and illustrated. Finally a number of alternate overall design strategies are evaluated and compared.

The central theme of the book is that thinking is a skill which must be acquired and developed. So many different types of thinking are called for in the design process that it is unlikely that the natural cognitive style of any one designer will be comprehensive and balanced. Thus it is necessary for students of design to identify and practise their less well developed thinking skills. The book is intended to assist in this learning process.

Illustrations:
Thanks are due to Cedric Green for the Sheffield University experimental solar house (fig. 10.3); Peter Cook for the Plug-in-city (fig. 6.2); Howell, Killich, Partridge and Amis for Bill Howell's drawings for University Centre, Cambridge (figs. 11.6, 11.7); Dr. Ing E. H. G. Lohmer, Architekt BDA, Köhn for drawings of Severin Bridge, Cologne (figs. 6.7, 6.8).

1 Introduction

To regard thinking as a skill rather than as a gift is the first step towards doing something to improve that skill.

Edward de Bono, *Practical Thinking*

Man's ability to perform skilled tasks is strongly affected by practice and by the degree to which he is motivated.

Fitts and Posner, *Human Performance*

Design education

"Design" has become one of those words having such a wide range of reference that we can no longer be really certain just what it means. In different contexts the word "design" can represent such varied situations that the underlying processes appear to share little in common. How is it that an engineer may be said to design a new gearbox for a car while a fashion designer may also be said to design a new dress? The process which gives rise to a new gearbox is surely precise, predetermined, systematic and mathematical in its nature! These are hardly the qualities associated with fashion design, which by contrast, seems rather nebulous, spontaneous, chaotic and imaginative. To make matters even more complicated many kinds of design call for a process which combines both these extremes in varying proportions. Town planning, urban design, architecture, industrial, graphic and interior design all involve elements which may seem both precise and nebulous, systematic and chaotic, mathematical and imaginative. These design fields all have to do with the creation of objects or places which have a practical purpose and which are intended both to be looked at and used.

All these areas fall somewhere near the centre of the spectrum of design activity. It is towards those studying this kind of design that this book is directed. Since architecture is one of the most centrally placed between the mathematical and the imaginative, and because the author is an architect, architectural examples will frequently be used to illustrate the principles discussed. However this is not a book about architecture, or indeed about any of the products of design. It is a book about design problems, and how to understand them, and about design processes and how to learn, develop and practise them.

Until quite recently designers relied almost exclusively on intuitive methods, and design ability was widely held to be innate and largely unteachable. The highly influential Beaux Arts school of design considered the most important set of factors contributing to the nature of the design situation to be those associated with the final outcome or end product. Under this system students were issued with schemes or projects which they took back to their studios to work on, only seriously contacting their tutors when they had completed the final drawings which were then criticised by juries. The schemes were graded for increasing complexity of solution, and indeed the project was described more as the task of producing a solution than of solving a problem. Thus the would-be architect might first be required to design a porch. When he had satisfied his tutors at this stage, he might be allowed to progress to a house and then a church and so on. In addition from time to time he had to produce measured drawings to develop his drafting and surveying skills, and "esquisses" or sketch designs to develop rapid design ability. Thus the educational emphasis was largely on product rather than process.

The inevitable reaction to such a philosophy generated a movement which sought more understanding of the design process itself. It was argued that the end product of design was too important a commodity for the process to remain such a neglected, hit and miss affair; society had a right to expect its designers to be responsible and accountable and have more control over their processes. Green (1974) summarises this argument by reminding us that the scale of operations in a technological society is such that individual design decisions can have such wide ranging effects as to render irresponsible the "accidentally inspired artistry" approach to design. Thus in the early nineteen sixties the time was right for a movement in design inspired by all the rational qualities of science, and the first generation of design methods came into being. Students would now be taught a systematic design method drawing heavily on the mathematical techniques of operations research and scientific method. After years of neglect when design methods had no place in the curriculum at all, they had now finally arrived in the textbook and lecture theatre.

This period, however, was not to last for long. Design proved too variable and complex a business to be amenable to such an inflexible approach. In the end perhaps design must be learnt rather than taught. We each of us have to acquire our own process, for it is we, not others, who must design with it. However, that process deserves extensive and careful study. To build a flexible and productive design process is neither a short nor an easy task and requires much painful self criticism and practice. It is hoped that this book may do a little to ease the pain.

Design technologies

Before we can make any real progress in developing a design process we must return to our first observation that design is a very varied sort of animal. It is easy enough to see that engineers and fashion designers are engaged in rather dissimilar forms of design. The real question is: just how different are their processes and why? Traditionally we tend to use the end products of design to differentiate between designers. Thus a client may go to one kind of designer for a bridge, another for a building, yet another for a chair and so on, but is this really necessary? Clegg (1969) shows how the inventive element of design is essentially independent of expert experience in a field. The following list of notable inventions and inventors nicely illustrates Clegg's point.

Invention	Inventor
Safety razor	Traveller in corks
Kodachrome films	Musician
Ballpoint pen	Sculptor
Automatic telephone	Undertaker
Parking meter	Journalist
Pneumatic tyre	Veterinary surgeon
Long-playing record	Television engineer

Classifying design by its end product seems to be rather putting the cart before the horse, for the solution is something which is formed by the design process and has not existed in advance of it. The real reason for classifying design in this way has very little to do with the design process but is instead a reflection of our increasingly specialised technologies. An engineer is different from an architect not just because he may use a different design process but more importantly because he understands about different materials and requirements. Unfortunately this sort of specialisation can easily become a straightjacket for the designer, directing his mental processes towards a predefined goal.

The cautionary tale of the scientist, the engineer, the artist and the church tower deals with just this problem. The three were standing outside the church arguing about the height of the tower when a local shopkeeper who was passing by suggested a competition. He was very proud of a new barometer which he now stocked in his shop and in order to advertise it he offered a prize to the one who could most accurately discover the height of the tower using one of his barometers. The scientist carefully measured the barometric pressure at the foot of the tower and again at the top, and from the difference he calculated the height. The engineer scorning this technique climbed to the top, dropped the barometer and timed the period of its fall. However it was the artist who to the surprise of all was the most accurate. He simply went inside the church and offered the barometer to the verger in exchange for allowing him to examine the original drawings of the church!

Many design problems are equally amenable to such varied treatment but seldom do clients have the foresight of our shopkeeper. Let us briefly examine such a situation. Imagine that a railway company has for many years been offering catering facilities only on certain trains and has now discovered that this part of the business is making a financial loss. What should be done? An advertising agency might suggest that they should design a completely new image with the food repackaged and differently advertised. An industrial designer might well suggest that the real problem is with the design of the buffet car. Perhaps if passengers were able to obtain and consume food in every coach they would buy more than if they had to walk down the train. An operations research consultant would probably turn his attention to whether the buffet cars were on the right trains; and so on.

It is quite possible that none of our professional experts was right. Perhaps the food was just not very appetising and too expensive? In fact, probably all the experts have something to contribute in designing a solution. The danger is that each may be conditioned by his own design technology. Design situations vary not just because the problems are dissimilar but also because designers habitually adopt different approaches. In this book we shall spend some time discussing both design problems and design approaches.

What does design involve?

It is obviously essential for a designer to have a good understanding of the technologies relevant to his field, but this alone will not make a successful and productive designer. Whitfield (1975) tells us how the famous inventor Barnes Wallis failed his London matriculation examination at the age of sixteen. As a result of undergoing a form of Armstrong's heuristic education at Christ's Hospital, Barnes Wallis recalls "I knew nothing, except how to think, how to grapple with a problem and then go on grappling with it until you had solved it." Later in life Barnes Wallis was quite prepared to take technical advice, but never accepted help with design itself. "If I wanted the answer to a question for which I could not do the mathematics I would go to someone who could ... to that extent I would ask for advice and help ... never a contribution to a solution." Even at an early age it was the quality of Barnes Wallis' thinking and his approach to problems as much as his technical expertise which enabled him to produce so many original aeronautical designs.

For many of the kinds of design we are considering it is important not just to be technically competent but also to have a well developed aesthetic appreciation. In environmental, product, or graphic design space, form, and line as well as colour and texture are the very tools of the trade. The end product of such design will always be visible to the user who may also move inside or pick up the designer's artifact. The designer must understand our aesthetic experience, particularly of the visual world, and in this sense his work may seem not unlike that of an artist. We must leave until later a discussion of why the practice of designing should not be considered as psychologically equivalent to the creation of art. Suffice it now to say that design demands more than just aesthetic appreciation. How many critics of design, even those with the most penetrating perception, find it easier to design than to criticise?

Perhaps there can be no exhaustive list of the areas of expertise needed by designers, but one major requirement remains unmentioned. The vast majority of the artifacts we design are created for particular groups of users. Designers must understand something of the nature of these users and their needs whether it be in terms of the ergonomics of chairs or the semiotics of graphics. Design education has come to recognise this rather obvious fact only relatively late in life and in recent years we have vocational design courses that begin to resemble degrees in behavioural and social sciences.

Yet the designer is no more a social scientist than he is an artist or a technologist. This book is not about science, art, or technology but the designer cannot escape the influences of these three very broad categories of intellectual endeavour. One of the essential difficulties and fascinations of designing is the need to embrace so many different kinds of thought and knowledge. The scientist may be able to do his job perfectly well without even the faintest notion of how an artist thinks, and the artist for his part certainly does not depend upon scientific method. For the designer life is not so simple, he must appreciate the nature of both art and science and in addition he must be able to design! What then exactly is this activity called design? That we must leave until the next chapter but we can already see that it involves a highly organised mental process capable of manipulating many kinds of information, blending them all into a coherent set of ideas and finally generating some realisation of those ideas. Usually this realisation takes the form of a drawing but, as we have seen it could equally well be a new timetable. In this book the word "design" refers not to the product but to the process.

Design as a skill

Design is a highly complex and sophisticated skill. It is not a mystical ability given only to those with recondite powers but a skill which, for many, must be learnt and practised rather like the playing of a sport or a musical instrument. Consider then the following two passages:

Flex the knees slightly and, while your upper body inclines towards the ball, keep from bending over too much at the waist. The arms are extended fully but naturally towards the ball without any great feeling of reaching out for the ball ... start the club back with that left arm straight, letting the right elbow fold itself against the body ... the head should be held over the ball ... the head is the fixed pivot about which the body and swing must function.

Lee Trevino (1972) *I Can Help Your Game*

Keeping the lips gently closed, extend them a little towards the corners as when half smiling, care being taken not to turn them inwards at all during the process. The "smile", rather a sardonic one perhaps, should draw in the cheeks against the teeth at the sides and the muscular action will produce a firmness of the lips towards the corners. Now, on blowing across the embouchure towards its outer edge, the breath will make a small opening in the middle of the lips and, when the jet of air thus formed strikes the outer edge the flute head will sound.

F. B. Chapman (1973) *Flute Technique*

These two passages come from books about skills; playing golf and playing the flute. They consist mainly of a series of suggestions as to where the learner should direct his attention. A few people may pick up a golf club and swing it naturally or easily sound a flute. For them these books may be of little help, but for the vast majority the skills must be acquired initially by attention to detail. It is in the very nature of highly developed skills that we can perform them unconsciously. The practiced golfer is not thinking about his swing but about the course, and the flautist will forget his embouchure and concentrate on the score. After all who could give expression to music while his mind was full of Chapman's advice about the lips? So it is with design. We probably work best when we think least about our technique. The beginner however must first analyse and practise all the elements of his skill and we should remember that even the most talented of professional golfers or musicians still benefit from lessons.

The famous British philosopher Ryle (1949) pronounced that "thought is very much a matter of drills and skills", and later the psychologist Bartlett (1958) proclaimed that "thinking should be treated as a complex and high level kind of skill". More recently there have been many writers who have exhorted their readers to practise this skill of thinking. One of the most notable, Edward de Bono (1968) summarises the message of such writers. "On the whole, it must be more important to be skilful in thinking than to be stuffed with facts."

We shall return to some relevant techniques of thinking once we have more thoroughly analysed the nature of design problems.

PART ONE

WHAT IS DESIGN?

2 The changing role of the designer in society

A bee puts to shame many an architect in the construction of her cells but what distinguishes the worst of architects from the best of bees is this, that the architect raises his structure in imagination before he erects it in reality. At the end of every labour process we get a result that already existed in the imagination of the labourer at its beginning.

Karl Marx, *Das Capital*

Vernacular or craft design

Design has not always been the professional activity it so often is today. In the industrialised world every article we buy has been designed by someone specifically trained to do just that. It was not always so, nor is it so now in many other societies. Recently a group of first year architecture students at Sheffield University were engaged on a number of simultaneous projects devised to stretch their design thinking skills. They were designing "machines" that would count and separate marbles, playing games simulating the roles of various members of the building design team and working with some computer-aided design programs. One day during these projects it snowed very heavily and the students spontaneously decided to abandon their work and instead they built an igloo in a nearby park. The igloo was very successful. It stood up well and could accommodate about ten people with the internal temperature rising considerably above that of the outside air. However what was so fascinating about this exercise was not so much the product but the process. The students immediately and without deliberation switched from the highly self-concious and introspective mode of thinking encouraged by their project work to a natural unselfconcious action-based approach.

There were no protracted discussions or disagreements about the form of the igloo, its siting, size, or even construction, and there were certainly no drawings produced. They simply got on and built it. In fact these students shared a roughly common image of an igloo in what we

2.1   Design students built an igloo without drawings

might fancifully describe as their collective consciousness. In this respect their behaviour bears a much greater resemblance to the Eskimo way of providing shelter than to the role of architect for which they were all being trained. Actually the common image of an igloo which these students shared and successfully realised was not entirely accurate in detail, for with their western preconceptions they built up the walls in courses whereas the Eskimo form of construction is usually a continuous spiral ramp.

As the igloo was completed the students' theoretical education began to take over again. There was much discussion about the compressive and tensile strength of compacted snow. The difficulties of building arches and vaulting with a material weak in tension were recognised. It was also realised that snow, even though it may be cold to touch, can be a very effective thermal insulator.

You would be unlikely to overhear such a discussion amongst Eskimos. Under normal conditions igloos are built in a vernacular manner. For the Eskimo there is no design problem but rather a traditional form of solution with variations to suit different circumstances which are selected and constructed without a thought of the principles involved.

In the past many objects have been consistently made to very

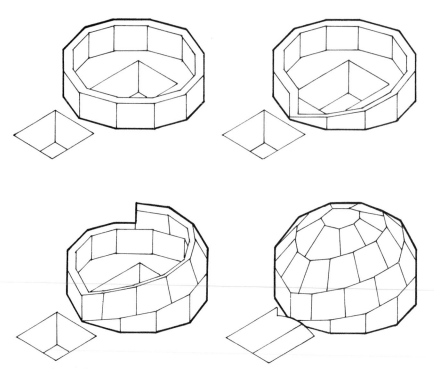

2.2 The traditional method of igloo construction

sophisticated designs with a similar lack of understanding of the theoretical background. This procedure is often referred to as "blacksmith design" after the craftsman who traditionally designed objects as he made them, working to undrawn traditional patterns handed down from generation to generation. There is a fascinating account of this kind of design to be found in George Sturt's (1923) book *The Wheelwright's Shop*. Sturt suddenly found himself in charge of a Wheelwright's shop in 1884 on the death of his father. In his book he recalls his struggle to understand what he describes as "a folk industry carried on in a folk method". Of particular interest here is the difficulty which Sturt found with the dishing of cartwheels. He quickly realised that wheels for horsedrawn vehicles were always constructed in a rather elaborate dished shape like that of a saucer, but the reason for this eluded Sturt. From his description we can see how Sturt's wheelwrights worked all their lives with the curious combination of constructional skill and theoretical ignorance that is so characteristic of such craftsmen. So Sturt continued the tradition of building such wheels for many years without really understanding why, but he was not content to remain in ignorance of the reasons behind the design. He

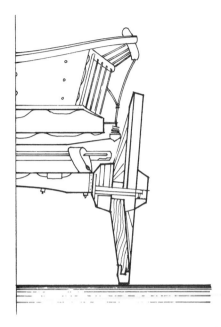

2.3 The cartwheel for horsedrawn vehicles was built with an elaborate dished geometry

first suspected that the dish was to give the wheel a direction in which to distort when the iron tyre was tightened on, but Jenkins (1972) has shown that dishing preceded the introduction of iron tyres. One other reason that occurred to Sturt was the advantage gained from the widening of the cart towards the top thus allowing overhanging loads to be carried. This could be achieved since that part of the dished wheel which transfers the load from axle to road must be vertical, and thus the upper half of the wheel leans outwards. This may have more validity than Sturt realised since legislation in 1773 restricted the track of broad wheeled vehicles to a maximum of 68". Although dished cartwheels were narrow enough to be exempt from this legislation the roads would have probably got so rutted by the broad wheeled vehicles that a cart with a wider track would have had to ride on rough ground.

Eventually Sturt discovered what he thought to be the "true" reason for dishing. The convex form of the wheel was capable not just of bearing the downward load but also the lateral thrust caused by the horse's natural gait which tends to throw the cart from side to side with each stride, but this is still by no means the total picture. Several writers have recently commented on Sturt's analysis and in particular Cross (1975) has pointed out that the dished wheel also needed foreway. To keep the bottom half of the wheel vertical the axle must slope down towards the wheel. In turn this produces a tendency for the wheel to slide off the axle which has to be countered by also pointing the axle

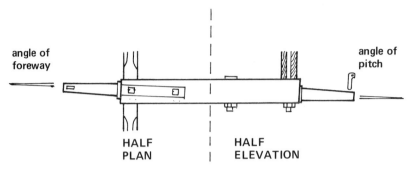

2.4   The axle had to be tilted down (pitch) to enable the cartwheel to transfer load through the spokes, and foreward (foreway) to prevent the cartwheel falling off

forward slightly thus turning the wheel in at the front. The resultant "foreway" forces the wheel back down the axle as the cart moves forwards. Cross seems to think this to be a forerunner of the toe-in used on modern cars to give them better cornering characteristics. This is not actually so, as Clegg (1969) has argued, since this modern toe-in is really needed to counter a lateral thrust caused by pneumatic rubber tyres not present in the solid cartwheel.

There probably is no one "true" reason for the dishing of cartwheels but rather a great number of interrelated advantages. This is very characteristic of the craft-based design process. After many generations of evolution the end product becomes a totally integrated response to the problem. Thus if any part is altered the complete system may fail in several ways. Such a process served extremely well when the problem remained stable over many years as with the igloo and the cartwheel. Should the problem suddenly change however the vernacular or craft process is unlikely to yield suitable results. If Sturt could not understand the principles involved in cartwheel dishing how would he have responded to the challenge of designing a wheel for a steam-driven or even a modern petrol-driven vehicle with pneumatic tyres?

The professionalisation of design
In the vernacular process designing is very closely associated with making. The Eskimos do not require an architect to design the igloo in which they live and George Sturt offered a complete design-and-build service to customers requiring wheels. In the modern western world things are often rather different. An average British house and its contents represent the end products of a whole galaxy of professionalised design processes. The house itself was probably

designed by an architect and sited in an area designated as residential by a town planner. Inside, the furnishings and fabrics, the furniture, the machinery and gadgets have all been created by designers who have probably never even once dirtied their hands with the manufacturing of these artifacts. The architect may have muddied his boots on the site when talking to the builder once in a while, but that is about as far as it goes. Why should this be? Does this separation of designing from making promote better design? We shall return to this question soon, but first we must examine the social context of this changed role for designers.

Approximately one in ten of the population of Great Britain may now be described as engaged upon a professional occupation. Most of the professions as we now know them are relatively recent phenomena and only really began to grow to their current proportions during the nineteenth century (Elliot 1972). The Royal Institute of British Architects was founded during this period. As early as 1791 there was an "Architects' Club" and later a number of Architectural Societies. The inevitable process of professionalisation had begun, and by 1834 the Institute of British Architects was founded. This body was no longer just a club or society but an organisation of like-minded men with aspirations to raise, control and unify standards of practice. The Royal Charter of 1837 began the process of acquiring social status for architects, and eventually the introduction of examinations and registration gave legal status. Indeed the very title architect is legally protected to this day. The whole process of professionalisation led inevitably to the body of architects becoming a legally protected and socially respected exclusive elite. The present remoteness of architects from builders and users alike was thus assured. For this reason many architects were unhappy about the formation of the RIBA, and there are still those today who argue that the legal barriers erected between designer and builder are not conducive to good architecture. Professionalism, however, was in reality not concerned with design or the design process but rather with the search for status and control, and can be seen amongst the design-based and non-design-based professions alike. Undoubtedly this control has led to increasingly higher standards of education and examination, but whether it has led to better practice is a more open question.

The division of labour between those who design and those who make has now become a keystone of our technological society. To some it may seem ironic that our very dependence on professional designers is largely based on the need to solve the problems created by the use of

2.5 The design of an isolated highland croft is a response to a stable problem

2.6 Each city centre site has its own particular complexities

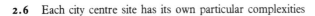

advanced technology. The design of a highland croft is a totally different proposition to the provision of housing in the noisy, congested city. The city centre site may bring with it social problems of privacy and community, risks to safety such as the spread of fire or disease, to say nothing of the problems of providing access or preventing pollution. The list of difficulties unknown to the builders of igloos or highland crofts is almost endless. Moreover each city centre site will provide a different combination of these problems. Such variable and complex situations seem to demand the attention of experienced professional designers who are not just technically capable but also trained in the act of design decision making itself.

Alexander (1964) has presented one of the most concise and lucid discussions of this shift in the designer's role. Alexander argues that the unselfconscious craft-based approach to design must inevitably give way to the selfconscious professionalised process when a society is subjected to a sudden and rapid change which is culturally irreversible. Such changes may be the result of contact with more advanced societies either in the form of invasion and colonisation or, as seen more recently, in the more insidious infiltration caused by overseas aid to the underdeveloped countries. In this country the Industrial Revolution provided such a change. The newly found mechanised means of production were to be the cultural pivot upon which society turned. The seeds of the nineteenth century respect for professions and the twentieth century faith in technology were sown. Changes in both the materials and technologies available became too rapid for the craftsman's evolutionary process to cope. Thus the design process as we have known it in recent times has come about not as the result of careful and wilful planning but rather as a response to changes in the wider social and cultural context in which design is practised. The professional specialised designer producing drawings from which others build has come to be such a stable and familiar image that we now regard this process as the traditional form of design.

The traditional design process

The questions we must then ask ourselves are how well has this new traditional design process served us and will it change? It has indeed always been undergoing a certain amount of change, and there are signs that many designers are now searching for a new, as yet ill-defined, role in society. Why should this be?

Initially the separating of designing from making had the effect not only of isolating the designer but also of making him the centre of attention. Alexander himself commented perceptively on this development. "The artist's self-conscious recognition of his individuality has a deep effect on the process of form-making. Each form is now seen as the work of a single man, and its success is his achievement only." This recognition of individual achievement can easily give rise to the cult of the individual. In educational terms it led to the articled pupillage system of teaching design. A young architect would put himself under the care of a recognised master of the art and hope that as the result of an extended period of this service he would acquire the skills peculiar to this individual master. Even in the schools of architecture students would be asked to design in the manner of a particular individual. To be successful designers had to acquire a clearly identifiable image, still seen in the flamboyant portrayal of designers in books and films. The great architects of the modern movement such as le Corbusier or Frank Lloyd Wright not only designed buildings with an identifiable style but also behaved and wrote eccentrically about their work. In this country those architects who were unhappy about the growing influence of the Royal Institute of British Architects in the late nineteenth century argued that architecture was an individual art and should not be regularised and controlled. Kaye (1960) argued that this period of professionalisation did actually coincide with a period of rigidity of architectural style.

Jones (1970) summarises both the strengths and weaknesses of this approach to design in a description of the process as "design by drawing." If the designer did not actually make an object then he had to represent it in another way. By far the most common and influential way of representing designs has been by drawing. The complete drawing of a design gave the designer great manipulative freedom. He could make alterations to parts of the solution and immediately see the implications. He could then continue this process of drawing and redrawing until all the problems he could see were resolved. This greater "perceptual span" (Jones 1970) enabled the designer to make more fundamental changes and innovations within one design than would ever have been possible in the vernacular process. Such a system worked well while design remained largely dominated by considerations of aesthetics. The designer could see from his drawing how the final solution would look. His model of reality was in this sense reasonably reliable and accurate.

The disadvantage of designing by drawing is that problems which are not visually apparent tend not to come to the designer's attention. Architects could not "see" the social problems associated with new forms of housing by looking at their drawings. Indeed such problems cannot easily be "seen" in the real world except in the form of such tell tales as graffiti and vandalism. It became apparent that if we were to continue separating designing from building, and also to continue the rapid rate of change and innovation, then new forms of modelling reality were urgently required.

It was precisely this concern that led Alexander to write his famous work *Notes on the Synthesis of Form* in 1964. He argued that we were far too optimistic in expecting anything like satisfactory results from a drawing board-based design process. How could a few hours or days of effort on the part of a designer replace the result of centuries of adaptation and evolution? Alexander proposed a method of structuring design problems that would allow designers to see a graphical representation of the structure of non-visual problems. This piece of work has had an extraordinarily lasting effect on thinking about design method. It is all the more remarkable since there is only one reported attempt to use the method and that did not result in any obvious success (Hanson 1969). In fact the reason for the failure of Alexander's method results from his erroneous assumptions about the true nature of design problems, and we shall discuss this in the next chapter. However that generation of design methodology for which Alexander's work now stands as a symbol was motivated by the common unease shared by designers about the inadequacy of their models of reality. Unfortunately the new models, which were frequently borrowed from operations research or behaviourist psychology, were to prove just as inadequate and inaccurate as designing by drawing (Daley 1969). Perhaps the real reason for the influence of Alexander's work was that it signalled yet another change in the designer's role. The issue no longer seemed to be one of protecting the individuality and identity of designers but rather had become the problem of exercising what Jones called "collective control" over the designers' activities. Somehow the whole process had to become more open to inspection and critical evaluation. The model of scientific method proved irresistible. Scientists made explicit not just their results but also their procedures. Their work could be replicated and criticised and their methods were above suspicion. This idea caused many writers to develop models of the design process itself and we shall examine some of these in the next section. But where does all this leave the designer's role in society today?

Future roles of the designer
In our current state of uncertainty it is hardly valid to give a definitive

view of the future or even present role of the designer. Cross (1975) asks us to consider whether we are now entering a post-industrial society and consequently in need of a post-industrial design process. The difficulty with this question is really how one views the prospect of life in such a post-industrial society. This issue is essentially a political debate about the extent to which we wish to decentralise the centres of power in our society. Some writers hail the looming energy crisis as providing the critical push towards a return to self sufficiency. Others claim that the inertia of our technological development is too great to be stopped and that we shall find other means of providing centralised forms of energy. Thus our views about the future role of designers are inevitably linked to the kind of direction in which we wish society to go. Markus (1972) suggests three broad views which designers today may hold about their role in society.

The first role is essentially conservative, centred around the continued dominance of the professional institutions. In such a role the designer remains unconnected with either clients or makers. He awaits the client's commission, produces his design and withdraws from the scene. There are already real problems with this approach. In the case of architecture the client is increasingly often some branch of government, and therefore architects become employees rather than professional consultants. We might expect that an architect seeking out this conservative role would be supported by the RIBA, but Elliot (1972) shows how professional bodies respond to threats against their roles by gradually redefining the role. Thus when the traditional role of building designer is threatened by obsolescence, changing technology or the changing nature of the clientele the architect may either seek to redefine himself as the leader of a multi-professional team or withdraw to his earlier territory of aesthetic and functional designer. It seems doubtful that a professional body such as the RIBA can continue for long to support both the general private practitioner and salaried government employee.

The opposite to this conservative approach is actively to seek changes in society which would result in the end of professionalism as we know it. Such a revolutionary approach would lead the designer to associate himself directly with user groups. Since this kind of designer is also likely to believe in a decentralised society he would be happiest when dealing with the disadvantaged, such as the tenants of slum clearance areas, or the revolutionary such as self sufficiency communes. In this role the designer deliberately foresakes his position of independence and power. He no longer sees himself as a leader but as a campaigner and spokesman. The difficulty with this role is that since the client/user group is unlikely to control any resources valued outside their limited society, the designer loses all influence over other designers except by the power of example.

The third, middle, path lies between these two extremes, and is much more difficult to identify except in vague terms. In this role the designer remains a professionally qualified specialist but tries to involve the users of his designs in his process. These more participatory approaches to design may include a whole range of relatively new techniques, ranging from the public inquiry through gaming and simulation to the recent computer-aided design procedures. All these techniques embody an attempt on the designer's part to identify the crucial aspects of the problem, make them explicit, and suggest alternative courses of action for comment by the non-designer participants. Designers following this approach are likely to have abandoned the traditional idea that the individual designer is dominant in the process, but they may still believe they have some specialised decision making skills to offer. We shall return to the problems created by this approach in two special sections on designing with others and with computers at the end of the book.

3 Descriptions of the design process

The six phases of a design project:
1 Enthusiasm
2 Disillusionment
3 Panic
4 Search for the guilty
5 Punishment of the innocent
6 Praise for the non-participants

Notice on the wall of the Greater London Council Architects Department. (According to Astragal AJ March 22 1978)

"Now for the evidence," said the King, "and then the sentence." "No!" said the Queen, "first the sentence, and then the evidence!" "Nonsense!" cried Alice, so loudly that everybody jumped, "the idea of having the sentence first!"

Lewis Caroll, *Alice Through the Looking Glass*

Do we need a definition of design?

This book did not begin with a definition of design but rather with an exploration of the variety and complexity of the designer's role. To attempt a definition of design too soon might easily lead to a narrow and restricted view. To understand fully the nature of design it is necessary not only to seek out the similarities between different design situations but also to recognise the very real differences. Inevitably, each of us will approach this general understanding of design from our own particular background. This is all too apparent when we attempt a comprehensive definition of design. What sort of designer might have offered the following definition? "The optimum solution to the sum of the true needs of a particular set of circumstances." Is it more likely that such a definition is the idea of an engineer or an interior designer? Is it meaningful to talk of "optimum solutions" or "true needs" in connection with interior design? In fact Matchett (1968), who defined design this way, comes from an engineering background. This definition suggests at least two ways in which design situations can vary. Matchett's use of "optimum" indicates that the results of design as he knows it can be measured against established criteria of success. This may well be the case for the design of a machine where output can be quantified on one or more scales of measurement, but it hardly applies to the design of a stage set or a building interior. Matchett's definition also assumes that all the "true needs" of a circumstance can be listed. More often than not however designers are by no means sure of all the needs of a situation. This is because not all design problems relate to equally purposeful activities. For example, it is much easier to define the needs to be satisfied in a lecture theatre than in a pub. Some pronouncements about design would have us believe that these differences are not really very important. "The process of design is the same whether it deals with the design of a new oil refinery, the construction of a cathedral or the writing of Dante's Divine Comedy" (Gregory 1966). If this were really the case then we might reasonably expect that Dante could have been a successful chemical engineer had he been alive today. Such statements about design, which have been common in recent years, deny the existence of any fundamental differences between the various design fields. The trouble with this approach is that it does not suggest that there is any discovering to be done. It is an intellectual dead end, and further inquiry into the nature of design is rendered unnecessary. Of course it is possible to arrive at a definition of design which allows for both the disparate and the common features. Jones (1970) gives what he regards to be the "ultimate" definition of design: "To initiate change in man-made things." All designers could probably agree that this applies to what they do, but does it really help? Surely such a definition is too general and abstract to be useful in helping us to understand design? Do we really need a simple definition of design or should we accept that design is too complex a matter to be summarised in less than a book? The answer is probably that we shall never really find a single satisfactory definition but that the searching is probably much more important than the finding. At least one well known thinker about design has publicly recognised just how difficult this search is in his description of design as: "The performing of a very complicated act of faith" (Jones 1966).

Some maps of the design process

One way of understanding more about design is to chart a route through the process from beginning to end. There have been many of these maps of the design process and we shall examine some of the most

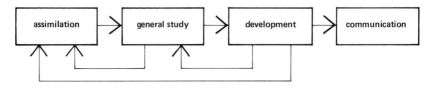

3.1   The RIBA plan of work map of the design process

frequently used routes in this section. In order to draw such a map we must observe the designer in action. One of the difficulties here is that on the whole there is not a great deal of action to be seen, and what there is cannot easily be understood. True, the designer may sketch or draw profusely but his drawings are by no means totally explicit about what is going on in his head. Unfortunately for those who would wish to draw a map therefore most of the route remains hidden, for it is what goes on in the designer's mind which really matters.

The first map we might examine is that laid out for use by architects in the RIBA practice and management handbook. The handbook tells us that the design process may be divided into four phases:

Phase 1   assimilation
The accumulation and ordering of general information and information specifically related to the problem in hand.

Phase 2   general study
The investigation of the nature of the problem.
The investigation of possible solutions or means of solution.

Phase 3   development
The development and refinement of one or more of the tentative solutions isolated during phase 2.

Phase 4   communication
The communication of one or more solutions to people inside or outside the design team.

The trouble with this is that it is hardly a map at all. As the handbook points out these four phases are not necessarily sequential although it may seem logical that the overall development of a design will progress from phase 1 to phase 4. Even a cursory logical examination of this map suggests that it is by no means a one way street and that there may have to be much coming and going. For example it is quite difficult to know what information to gather in phase 1 until you have done some investigation of the problem in phase 2. Since the introduction of systematic design methods into design education it has become fashionable to require students to prepare reports accompanying their designs. Frequently such reports contain a great deal of information, slavishly gathered at the beginning of the project, which has no material effect upon the solution. One of the dangers here is that since gathering information is rather less mentally demanding than solving problems there is always a temptation to put off the transition from phase 1 to phase 2. Then again the detailed development of solutions (phase 3) does not always go smoothly and may sometimes suggest that more general study is required (phase 2). In short all this map does is to tell us that designers have to gather information about a problem, study it, devise a solution and draw it, though not necessarily in that order. The RIBA Handbook is very honest here in declaring that there are likely to be unpredictable jumps between the four phases. What it does not tell us is how often or in what way these jumps are made.

If we turn on through the pages of the RIBA Handbook there is yet another, much larger scale map to be found. Because of its immense detail (it occupies 27 A4 pages) this Plan of Work, as it is called, looks much more promising at first sight. The plan of work consists of twelve stages described as a logical course of action.

A   Inception
B   Feasibility
C   Outline proposals
D   Scheme design
E   Detail design
F   Production information
G   Bills of quantities
H   Tender action
J   Project planning
K   Operations on site
L   Completion
M   Feed-back

The handbook rather revealingly also shows a simplified version in what it describes as "usual terminology".

A–B   Briefing
C–D   Sketch plans
E–H   Working Drawings
J–M   Site operations

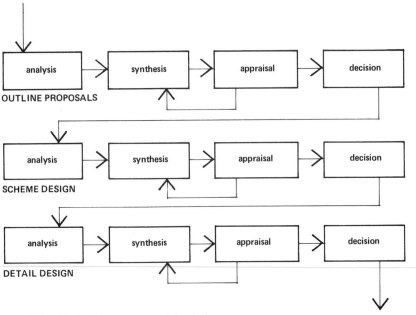

3.2   The Markus/Maver map of the design process

From this we can see the Plan of Work for what it really is; a description not of the process but of the products of that process. It tells us not how the architect works but rather what he produces in terms of feasibility reports, sketch plans, production drawings, and what he does in terms of obtaining planning approval and supervising the construction of the building. It is also worth noting that the stages in the Plan of Work are closely related to the stages of fee payment in the Conditions of Engagement for Architects. So the Plan of Work may also be seen as part of a business transaction; it tells the client what he will get, and the architect what he must do rather than how it is done. In the detailed description of each section the Plan of Work also describes what each member of the design team (quantity surveyor, engineers etc) will do, and how he will relate to the architect; with the architect clearly portrayed as the manager and leader of this team. This further reveals the Plan of Work to be part of the architectural profession's propaganda exercise to stake a claim as leader of the multi-disciplinary building design team. None of this should be taken as criticism of the RIBA Plan of Work, which probably performs its functions quite adequately, but in the end we probably learn from it more about the role of the RIBA than about the nature of architectural design processes.

Markus (1969) and subsequently Maver (1970) have developed and related these two RIBA maps of designing. They argue that a complete picture of design method requires both a "decision sequence" and a "design process" or "morphology". Markus and Maver suggest that we need to go through the decision sequence of analysis, synthesis, appraisal, and decision at increasingly detailed levels of the design process (stages 2, 3, 4, 5 in the RIBA Handbook). Since the concepts of analysis, synthesis, and evaluation or appraisal occur frequently in the literature on design methodology it is worth attempting some rough definitions. Analysis involves the exploration of relationships, looking for patterns in the information available, and the classification of objectives. Essentially analysis is the ordering and structuring of the problem. Synthesis on the other hand is characterised by an attempt to move forward and create a response to the problem. Essentially, synthesis is the generating of solutions. Appraisal involves the critical evaluation of suggested solutions against the objectives identified in the analysis phase.

To see how these three functions of analysis, synthesis, and evaluation are related in practice we might examine the thoughts of a chess player deciding on his next move. The procedure suggests that first our player might analyse the current position on the board by studying all the relations between the pieces; the pieces that are being threatened and how, and which of the unoccupied squares remain unguarded.

The next task would be to clarify objectives. Obviously the ultimate long term object of the game is to win, but at this particular stage the priorities between attack or defence and between immediate or eventual gain have to be decided. The synthesis stage would be to suggest a move, which might emerge either as a complete idea or in parts, such as moving a particular piece, occupying a particular square or threatening a particular piece, and so on. This idea then needs evaluating against the objectives.

Our map of the design process must allow for an indefinite number of return loops from evaluation to synthesis. The first move thought of by our chess player may on examination prove unwise or even dangerous, and so it is with design. This accounts for the return loop in the Markus/Maver decision sequence from appraisal to synthesis, which in simple terms calls for the designer to get another idea.

The presence of this return loop in the diagram however raises another question. Why is it the only return loop? Might not the development of a solution suggest more analysis is needed? Even in the

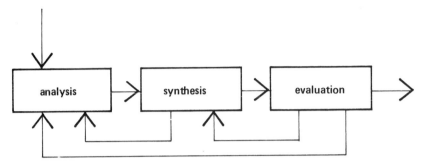

3.3   Even the simplest map of the design process must allow for a return loop to all preceding functions

game of chess a proposed move may reveal a new problem and suggest that the original perception of the state of the game was incomplete and that further analysis is necessary. This is even more frequently the case in design where the problem is not totally described, as on a chess board. This was long ago recognised by Page (1963) who warned the 1962 Conference on Design Methods at Manchester, "In the majority of practical design situations, by the time you have produced this and found out that and made a synthesis, you realise you have forgotten to analyse something else here, and you have to go round the cycle and produce a modified synthesis, and so on." So we are inevitably led to the conclusion that our map should actually show a return loop from each function to all preceding functions.

The map, such as it is, no longer suggests any firm route through the whole process. It rather resembles one of those chaotic party games where the players dash from one room of the house to another simply in order to discover where they must go next. It is about as much help in navigating a designer through his task as a diagram showing how to walk would be to a one year old child. Knowing that design consists of analysis, synthesis and evaluation linked in an iterative cycle will no more enable you to design than knowing the movements of breaststroke will prevent you from sinking in a swimming pool. You will just have to put it all together for yourself.

So much space has been devoted to maps of design because they occur so frequently in the literature. Many writers fail to point out that such maps are probably much more use to the methodologist than to the designer. Indeed they have proved invaluable in provoking a continued study of the design process. At this level of abstraction there is an extraordinarily high degree of agreement between designers in different fields, this suggesting that we are indeed discussing a process which can

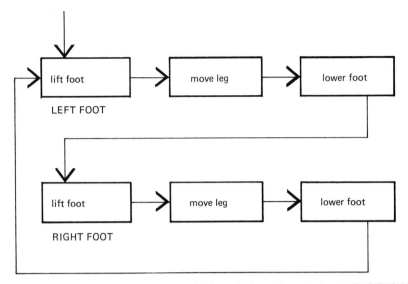

3.4   A map of the "walking process" (with apologies to those design methodologists who like maps!)

be studied independently of the various technical contexts in which it is practised. Maps of design very similar to those already mentioned have been proposed by engineers (Asimow 1962; and Rosenstein, Rathbone and Schneerer 1964), industrial designers (Archer 1963) and workers in the field of town planning (Levin 1966), as well as by many other architects. In the next section we will see something of how designers actually navigate through the process in practice.

Do we really need to use a map?

We have now seen a few of the many maps of the design process which have been drawn up in recent years by design methodologists. These maps tend to be both theoretical and prescriptive. They seem to have been derived more by thinking about design than by experimentally observing it, and characteristically they are logical and systematic. For example neither the RIBA Handbook nor Markus produce any evidence to show that designers actually behave as if they were reading such maps. We are simply told that this is how design goes as the writers see it. There is a danger with this approach, since writers on design methodology do not necessarily always make the best designers, and that must obviously include this author too. It seems reasonable to suppose that our best designers are more likely to spend their time designing than writing about methodology. In which case we are entitled to ask how valid is a design methodologist's view of the process? Surely he sees design with a rather special perspective? In fact many writers about design have not only trained as designers themselves but are also involved in teaching design. Their thoughts are based not just on their own knowledge of design but also on their experience of observing students struggling to acquire and develop design skills.

There is another way out of this difficulty. In recent years we have begun to study design in a more organised and scientific way. Studies have been and are being conducted in which designers are put under the microscope, and from this research we are gradually learning something of the subtleties of design as it is actually practised. We shall now examine some of this work to see the picture which is gradually emerging.

One of the major questions to be answered here is whether or not designers come to adopt a recognisably consistent approach to design problems. Do all designers use similar strategies or, alternatively, are there as many ways of tackling a problem as there are designers? Lawson (1972) set out to explore this issue in a series of experiments in which various groups, both of designers and non-designers, were asked to solve design-like problems. In one experiment Lawson (1979a) compared the strategies of final year architectural students and science students at a similar stage of post-graduate education. In order not to give the architects a technical advantage an experimental task was devised which did not demand any specialist expertise. In this case the problem was to arrange some modular coloured wooden blocks onto a four by three bay rectangular plan. There were eight blocks, two of each of four different shapes and each with some faces coloured red and some blue. The objective was to so arrange the blocks that either as much red or as much blue as possible was left showing around the external face of the finished design. Only four blocks of the eight, one of each different shape were to be used. In addition, for each problem certain combinations of block were permitted while others were not. These allowed combinations were governed by a simple rule which might require one particular block to be present or alternatively at least one of two specified blocks to be present and so on. While the subjects were aware of the existence of this rule they were not told of its nature. They were, however, allowed to submit designs and were then told whether their solutions were acceptable or not. The subject was not given a time limit and was asked to decide for himself when he thought he had got the best solution possible and to arrive at this by submitting as few designs as he could.

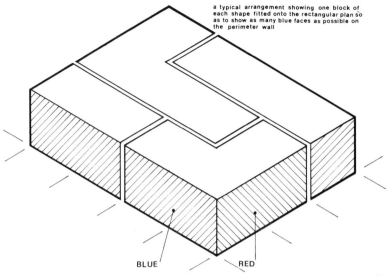

a typical arrangement showing one block of
each shape fitted onto the rectangular plan so
as to show as many blue faces as possible on
the perimeter wall

BLUE   RED

3.5   Lawson's (1972) experimental apparatus

Thus this abstract problem is in reality a very simplified design situation where a physical three-dimensional solution has to achieve certain stated performance objectives while obeying a relational structure which is not entirely explicit at the outset. The question was how would the designers and non-designers approach this problem. Would any discernable strategies emerge which might reveal something of the way each group or person was thinking?

The two groups showed quite consistent and strikingly different strategies. Although this problem is simple compared with most real design problems there are still over six thousand possible answers. Clearly then the immediate task facing the subjects was how to narrow this number down and search for an optimal solution. The scientists adopted a technique of trying out a series of designs which used as many different blocks and combinations of blocks as possible as quickly as possible. Thus they tried to maximise the information available to them about the problem. If they could discover the rule governing which combinations of blocks were allowed they could then search for an arrangement which would optimise the required colour around the design.

The architects on the other hand selected their blocks in quite a different way. The eight blocks were examined to see which four blocks had the most of the desired colour, and the first design was built from these four blocks. If this proved not to be an acceptable combination then the next most favourably coloured block would be substituted and so on until an acceptable solution was discovered.

The essential difference between these two strategies is that while the scientists focused their attention on discovering the rule, the architects were obsessed with achieving the desired result. The scientists adopted a generally problem-focused strategy and the architects a solution-focused strategy. Although it would be quite possible using the architects' approach to achieve the best solution without actually discovering the complete range of acceptable solutions, in fact most architects discovered something about the rule governing the allowed combinations of blocks. In other words they learnt about the nature of the problem largely as a result of trying out solutions, whereas the scientists set out specifically to study the problem.

Most of the maps of the design process which we have looked at seem to resemble more closely the non-designer, scientist approach than that of the architects: first analysis and then synthesis. For the designers it seems, analysis, or understanding the problem is much more integrated with synthesis, or generating a solution. Why should this be? Is it that designers are just a different sort of person to scientists, is it the result of their education, or is it something to do with the different nature of the problems they normally solve?

Groups of first year architectural students and sixth year pupils took part in the same experiment. Both groups performed significantly worse than the postgraduate students and neither group showed any consistent problem-solving strategy. The results of these experiments tend to suggest that design students do not naturally have a consistent approach to problems but that they seem to acquire one during their education. It could be argued that the two postgraduate student groups in this experiment had developed strategies that reflected the educational methods they had undergone. An architect is taught mainly by example and practice. He is judged by the solutions he produces rather than the methods by which he arrives at those solutions. Not so the scientist who is taught a succession of concepts and methods of demonstrating the validity of those concepts. He is exercised by examples only in order to demonstrate that he can apply the principles he has learnt. However this is perhaps too simple an explanation. Although their performance was no better overall, both groups of design students showed greater skill than their peers in actually forming the three-dimensional solutions. They appeared to have greater spatial ability and to be more interested in simply playing around with the blocks. Is it then possible that the respective educational systems used for science and architecture simply reinforce an interest in the abstract or the concrete?

In a slightly more realistic experiment Eastman (1970) asked more experienced designers to redesign a bathroom for speculatively-built houses. Eastman recorded what his designers did and said about what they were doing. From these protocols Eastman showed how the designers explored the problem through a series of attempts to create solutions. There is no meaningful division to be found between analysis and synthesis in these protocols but rather a simultaneous learning about the nature of the problem and the range of possible solutions. The designers were supplied with an existing bathroom design together with some potential clients' criticisms of the apparent waste of space. Thus some parts of the problem, such as the need to reorganise the facilities so as to give a greater feeling of spaciousness and luxury, were quite clearly stated. However the designers discovered much more about the problem as they critically evaluated their own solutions. One of Eastman's protocols shows how a designer came to identify the problem of shielding the toilet from the bath for reasons of privacy. Later this becomes part of a much more subtle requirement as he decides that the client would not like one of his designs which seems deliberately to hide the toilet, the toilet then is to be shielded but not hidden. This requirement was not thought out in the abstract and stated in advance of synthesis but rather discovered as a result of manipulating solutions.

Darke (1978) has also found this tendency to structure design problems by exploring aspects of possible solutions. She interviewed some well known British architects about their intentions when designing local authority housing. The architects first discussed their views on housing in general and how they saw the problems of designing such housing and then discussed the history of a particular housing scheme in London. In fact the design of housing under these conditions presents an extremely complex problem. The range of legislative and economic controls, the subtle social requirements and the demands of London sites all interact to generate a highly constrained situation. Faced with all this complexity Darke shows how the architects tended to latch onto a relatively simple idea very early in the design process. This idea, or primary generator as Darke calls it, may be to create a mews-like street or leave as much open space as possible and so on. For example one architect described how "... we assumed a terrace would be the best way of doing it ... and the whole exercise, formally speaking, was to find a way of making a terrace continuous so that you can use space in the most efficient way ...". Thus a very simple idea is used to narrow down the range of possible solutions, and the designer is then able rapidly to construct and analyse a scheme. Here again we see

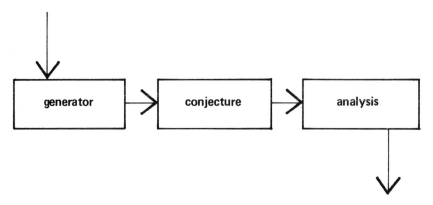

3.6   Darke's partial map of the design process

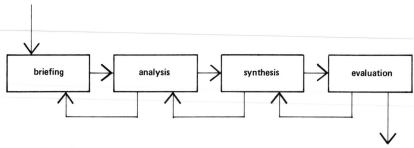

3.7   Even the briefing stage needs to be accessible by return loops

this very close, perhaps inseparable, relation between analysis and synthesis. Darke however uses her empirically-gained evidence to propose a new kind of map which owes a great deal to another theoretically derived map by Hillier et al (1972). Instead of analysis-synthesis Darke's map reads generator-conjecture-analysis. In plain language, first decide what you think might be an important aspect of the problem, develop a crude design on this basis and examine it to see what else you can discover about the problem.

We shall return to this idea again in a later section but before we leave Darke's work it is worth noting some other evidence that she presents with little comment but which even further calls into question the RIBA Handbook kind of design process map. One of the architects interviewed was explicit about his method of obtaining a design brief (stages A and B in the RIBA Handbook) " ... a brief comes about through essentially an ongoing relationship between what is possible in architecture and what you want to do, and everything you do modifies your idea of what is possible ... you can't start with a brief and (then)

roughly hierarchically. It is rarely possible to discern precisely how far above the stated problem one should begin and how far below one should call a halt. Creatively uncovering the range of his problem is one of the designer's most important skills, and we shall look at some problem identification techniques in chapter 12.

The structure of design problems

Design problems are often both multidimensional and highly interactive. Very rarely does any part of a designed thing serve only one purpose. The American architect Philip Johnson is reported to have observed that some people find chairs beautiful to look at because they are comfortable to sit in, while others find chairs comfortable to sit in because they are beautiful to look at. Certainly no one can deny the importance of both of the visual and ergonomic aspects of chair design. The legs of a stacking upright chair present an even more multidimensional problem. The geometry and construction of these chair legs must provide stability and support, allow for interlocking when stacked and be sympathetic to the designer's visual intentions for the chair as a whole. The designer of such a chair is unlikely to succeed by thinking separately about the problems of stability, support, stacking and visual line since all must be satisfied by the same element of the solution. In fact the designer must also be aware of other more general problems such as cost and manufacturing limitations, the availability of materials and the durability of finishes and joints.

In design then it is frequently necessary to devise an integrated solution to a whole cluster of requirements. We saw in the second chapter how George Sturt's dished cartwheel provided such an integrated response to structural, mechanical, and even legislative demands. In buildings the window is another unavoidably multidimensional component. As well as letting in daylight and sunlight the window is also usually required to provide a view while retaining privacy, and to offer natural ventilation. As an interruption in the external wall the window also poses problems of structural stability, heat loss and noise transmission, and is thus arguably one of the most complex of building elements. Modern science can be used to study each of the many problems of window design with branches of physics, psycho-physics and psychology all being relevant. This is indeed a complex array of concepts to lay before an architect. Most courses in architecture do attempt to teach most of this scientific material. However the methods of science are perhaps surprisingly unhelpful to the designer. Modern building science techniques have only been able

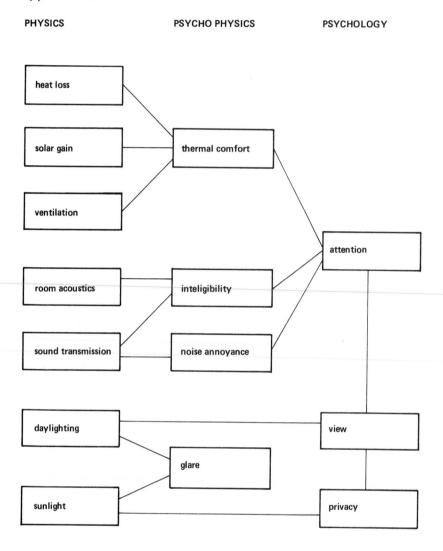

PHYSICS **PSYCHO PHYSICS** **PSYCHOLOGY**

heat loss

solar gain — thermal comfort

ventilation

attention

room acoustics — inteligibility

sound transmission — noise annoyance

daylighting — view

glare

sunlight — privacy

4.2   Some of the problems involved in window design

to provide methods of predicting how well a design solution will work. They are simply tools of evaluation and give no help at all with the design. Daylight protractors, heat loss or solar gain calculations do not tell the architect how to design his window but rather help him to assess the performance of an already designed window. Jones (1970) summarises how Page, a professor of building science, proposes that designers should adopt what he calls a cumulative strategy for design in such a situation. This would involve setting carefully defined objectives and criteria of success for the performance of the window on all the dimensions we have identified. Page's strategy then calls for the designer to collect a variety of what he calls sub-solutions for each criterion and then discard the solutions which fail to satisfy all the criteria. Thus the window designer would produce a succession of designs, some intended to achieve a good view, others to avoid solar gain or good daylighting and so on. We are told that this strategy is intended to increase the amount of time spent on analysis and synthesis and reduce the time spent on the synthesis of bad solutions.

It is interesting that this strategy, suggested by a scientist, resembles the behaviour of the science students in Lawson's experiment described in the last chapter. Such an approach however does not seem borne of a clear understanding of the true nature of design problems. Because design problems are so multidimensional they are also highly interactive. Enlarging our window may well let in more light and give a better view but this will also result in more heat loss and may create greater problems of privacy. It is the very interconnectedness of all these factors which is the essence of design problems rather than the isolated factors themselves. In this respect designing is rather like devising a crossword. Change the letters of one word and several other words will need altering necessitating even further changes. Modify the dish of George Sturt's cartwheel and it may fail to support its load and the lateral thrusts unless the angle of toe in and axle mounting are also changed. After this the cart may not fit the rutted roads unless the length of the axle and shape of the body are changed. As we have seen, the cartwheel was the result of many years of experience rather than theoretical analysis. Until the advent of modern building science this is just how windows were designed. Perhaps the finest period for window design in England was the eighteenth century. The vertical proportions of Georgian windows positioned near the outer edge of the wall and with splayed or stepped reveals gave excellent daylight penetration and distribution. The vertical sliding sash was reasonably weatherproof and gave much more flexible ventilation configurations than the casement which was to replace it. The proportions of solid wall and window, so fundamental to the late renaissance, worked well structurally, gave an even light and offered privacy for those behind. Above all, of course, the Georgian window was integrated into a superb architectural language and it seems unlikely that the eighteenth century architect would have been distressed by his lack of expertise in building science. However if the modern designer is going to abandon traditional or vernacular solutions he cannot afford to remain so ignorant of the

4.3 The Georgian window offers a beautifully integrated solution to the problems in fig. 4.2

structure of his problems as the renaissance architect or George Sturt. As Chermayeff and Alexander (1963) put it:

Too many designers miss the fact that the new issues which legitimately demand new forms are there, if the pattern of the problems could only be seen as it is and not as the bromide image (of a previous solution) conveniently at hand in the catalogue or magazine around the corner.

This "pattern of the problem" is comprised of all the interactions between one requirement and another which constrain what the designer may do. Chermayeff and Alexander again: "... every problem has a structure of its own. Good design depends upon the designer's ability to act according to this structure and not to run arbitrarily counter to it." We can observe some general rules about the nature of this pattern of constraints in design and we shall discuss these in a later chapter. First however, we need to look more carefully at the way the performance of designs can be measured against criteria of success.

5 Measurement, criteria and judgement in design

"She can't do Substraction," said the White Queen. "Can you do Division? Divide a loaf by a knife – what's the answer to that?" "I suppose –" Alice was beginning, but the Red Queen answered for her. "Bread-and-butter of course."

Lewis Carroll, *Alice Through the Looking Glass*

Measurement

Learning and developing a good design process is not an end in itself, but hopefully just a step towards producing better designs. In the final analysis it is the solution not the process which matters in design. But how can the degree of success achieved by a design solution be measured? Is it possible to say that one design is better than another and if so by how much? Such questions are not so easily answered as it may appear on first examination.

Consider the design of a garden greenhouse. There are a number of features which the designer of a greenhouse can vary. He could choose between several different materials for the frame; perhaps wood, steel, aluminium or plastic. The actual form of the greenhouse is even more variable with possibilities of domes, tent shapes, barrel vaults and so on. In fact there are many more design variables including the glazing material, method of ventilation and type of door. What the designer has to do is to select the combination of all these features which will give the most satisfactory performance. How then do we measure the performance of our greenhouse? A greenhouse is designed for one fairly clear and simple purpose; to trap heat from the sun, so we can begin by measuring or calculating the thermal efficiency of a whole range of possible greenhouses. Unfortunately, we are still some way from describing how satisfactory our greenhouse will appear to a gardener. He may well also want to know how much it will cost to buy, how long it will last, or how easy it will be to erect and maintain, and perhaps, what it will look like in his garden. The greenhouse then, must

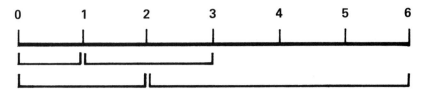

0   1   2   3   4   5   6

Ratios are equal e.g. 3:1 = 6:2

5.1   The ratio scale of measurement

$$10 : 5 = 2.0$$

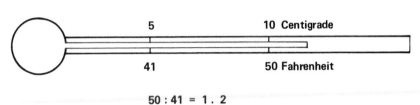

5   10 Centigrade

41   50 Fahrenheit

$$50 : 41 = 1.2$$

5.2   On thermometers, temperature is obviously not a ratio scale since the ratios of two temperatures are different in centigrade and fahrenheit

satisfy criteria of solar gain, cost, durability, ease of assembly, appearance and perhaps many others. It is quite likely that these criteria are not all equally important but the real difficulty here is that neither are they easily related one to another. It is obviously relatively easy to measure solar gain or durability, but what about ease of assembly or appearance? Measurement in design apparently involves both quantities and qualities. Somehow then, designers must be able to balance both qualitative and quantitative criteria in their decision making process.

In every day life we tend to use numbers and scales of measurement very carelessly. In fact we commonly employ several quite distinct ways of using numbers, without really being aware of the differences. Designers cannot afford to be so careless since they must frequently use all these different kinds of measurement scales simultaneously. We normally tend to assume that numbers are organised along what is usually called a ratio scale which is the normal language of counting where four represents twice two. However this is not always the case, for example while four apples certainly are twice as many as two apples, ten degrees centigrade are not twice as hot as five degrees centigrade. Why this should be can be seen by using both our common temperature scales together. One temperature described as 10° centigrade can also

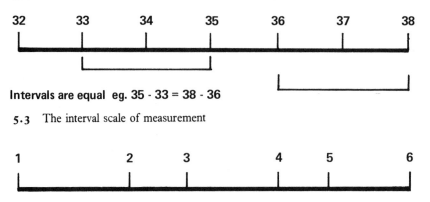

Intervals are equal eg. 35 - 33 = 38 - 36

5.3   The interval scale of measurement

Numbers in ascending order e.g. 5 greater than 4

5.4   The ordinal scale of measurement

be described as 50° fahrenheit, and a lower temperature of 5° centigrade corresponds to 41° fahrenheit. Thus these two temperatures give a ratio of 10 to 5 or 2 to 1 on the centigrade scale, but a ratio of 50 to 41 on the fahrenheit scale. This is because the zero point on these scales is not absolute but entirely arbitrary. The centigrade scale is actually defined as having one hundred equal intervals between the freezing and boiling temperatures of water. We could equally easily use a thousand intervals or the freezing and boiling temperatures of any other substance. These temperature scales are described as interval measurement. Although 10°C cannot be described as twice as hot as 5°C the difference, or interval, between 0°C and 5°C is exactly equal to the interval between 5°C and 10°C. Interval scales are frequently used for subjective assessment. Psychologists recommend that such scales should be fairly short, up to seven intervals, to retain the reliability of the interval. Thus to return to our greenhouse, we might ask a number of gardeners to assess the ease of assembly or maintenance on five point scales. We would not be justified in regarding a greenhouse assessed as 4 for assembly as being twice as easy to assemble as one assessed as only 2.

Sometimes we use an even more cautious scale of measurement where the interval is not considered to be reliably consistent. Such scales are called ordinal, for they represent only a sequence or order. Cars in a traffic queue are arranged along an ordinal scale. We make no guarantee of the size of gap between each car, when we describe a particular car as fourth or fifth in the queue. The winners of a race are

5.5   The nominal scale of measurement

described as first, second and third, but this does not tell us how large were the gaps between them. Regulations require that the materials used in buildings should not allow flame to spread across their surface in case of fire. Materials can belong to one of five surface spread of flame classes which range from class 0 to class 4. On this ordinal scale the higher the number the more rapidly flame will spread, but the difference between class 1 and class 2 is not necessarily the same as the difference between class 2 and class 3. We also get ordinal scales when we ask people to rank order their preferences. Thus we could ask our gardeners to put a number of greenhouses in order of attractiveness of appearance. Whether ordinal or interval scales of assessment are appropriate remains a matter of judgement, but generally ordinal scales should be used where the assessment may depend on many factors or where the factors cannot easily be defined. Thus while it seems reasonable to ask our gardeners how much easier it is to assemble one greenhouse than another, it does not seem reasonable to ask how much more attractive it may be. Academic examiners may award marks out of one hundred for a particular examination, which is really an interval scale since the zero point is rarely used. Overall degree classifications however are usually based on the cruder ordinal scale of first, upper and lower second, third and pass.

Finally the fourth, least precise numbering system in common use is the nominal scale, so called because the numbers really represent names and cannot be manipulated arithmetically. The numbers on football players' shirts are nominal. A forward is neither better nor worse than a back and two goal keepers do not make a full back. In fact there is no sequence or order to these numbers, we could equally easily have used the letters of the alphabet or any other set of symbols.

The importance of understanding these scales of measurement lies in the recognition that they must each be used in different ways. The inappropriate use of too precise a scale or arithmetic may lead to misleading results and false conclusions in design. One of the most well-known cases of such a confusion between scales of measurement is to be found in Archer's (1969) highly elaborate and numerical model of the design process. Archer, apparently somewhat reluctantly, concedes that at least some assessment of design must be subjective, but since he sets up a highly organised system of measuring satisfaction in design Archer clearly wants to use only ratio scales. Archer argues that a scale of 1–100 can be used for subjective assessment and the data then treated as if it were on a true ratio scale. In this system a judge, or arbiter as Archer calls him, is asked not to rank order or even to use a short interval scale, but to award marks out of 100. Archer argues that if the arbiters are correctly chosen and the conditions for judgement are adequately controlled, such a scale could be assumed to have an absolute zero and constant intervals. Archer does not specify how to "correctly choose" the judges or "adequately control the conditions," and his argument does seem rather suspect. In fact Stevens (1951), who originally defined the rules for measurement scales, did so to discourage psychologists from exactly this kind of numerical dishonesty. It is interesting to note that psychology itself was then under attack in an age of logic as being too imprecise to deserve the title of science. Perhaps for this reason, many psychologists had been tempted to treat their data as if it were more precise than Stevens' rules would indicate. Archer's work seems a parallel attempt to force design into a scientifically respectable mould. It now seems, some years later, that this attempt has failed and it is important to understand just why Stevens' rules for measurement scales should be respected in design as much as in psychology.

Value judgement and criteria

It is frequently tempting to employ more apparently accurate methods of measurement in design than the situation really deserves. Not only do the higher level scales, ratio and interval, permit much more arithmetic manipulation, but they also permit absolute judgement to be made. If it can be shown that, under certain circumstances 20°C is found to be a comfortable temperature then that value can be used as an absolutely measurable criterion of acceptability. Life is not so easy when ordinal measurement must be used. Universities use external examiners to help protect and preserve the "absolute" value of their degree classifications. It is, perhaps, not too difficult for an experienced examiner to rank order his pupils, but much more difficult to maintain a constant standard over many years of developing curricula and changing examinations. It is tempting to avoid these difficult problems of judgement by instituting standardised procedures. Thus, to continue the example, a computer-marked multiple choice question examination technique might be seen as a step towards more reliable assessment. But there are invariably disadvantages with such techniques. Paradoxically, conventional examinations allow examiners to tell much more accurately, if not entirely reliably, how much their students have actually understood.

It is easy to fall into the trap of over-precision in design. Students of architecture sometimes submit thermal analyses of their buildings with the rate of heat loss through the building fabric calculated down to the last watt. Ask them how many kilowatts are lost when a door is opened and they are incapable of answering. Daylight design has been the subject of perhaps the most absurd series of measurement misconceptions. We all know that the level of natural illumination varies considerably throughout the day and even from minute to minute if the sun is periodically obscured by clouds. Normally this is relatively unimportant since the human eye is able to accommodate a very wide range of illumination. In fact the ratio of the brightest to the dimmest levels of illumination at which the human eye works efficiently is about 100,000 : 1. However this appears to be too untidy for building scientists who have invented the concept of a standard overcast sky. In this notional sky brightness is uniform all round the compass but greater at the zenith than the horizon, and there is no awkward sun. Such an abstraction permits the calculation of the percentage of total illumination from this theoretical sky which is available at a particular point in a room. Because these calculations involve very complex solid geometry the designer can easily be misled into believing that he has arrived at an absolute and meaningful result. Nothing could be further from the truth. In fact the daylight factor can only be used to compare one point with another on paper, it tells very little about the actual experience of being in the room in question. The danger of such techniques is that sooner or later they get used as fixed criteria. In fact this actually happened in the case of daylighting. Using statistics of the actual levels of illumination expected over the year it was calculated that a 2 per cent daylight factor was desirable in schools. It then became a mandatory requirement that all desks in new schools receive at least this daylight factor. The whole geometry of the classrooms themselves was thus effectively prescribed and, as a result, a generation of schools were built with large areas of glazing. The resultant acoustic and visual distraction, glare, draughts, the colossal heat losses and excessive solar gain in summer, which were frequently experienced in these schools,

Worktop   sink   worktop   cooker   worktop

sequence to be unbroken by door or traffic way

5.6 A mandatory design requirement does not allow the designers to make a value judgement

eventually led to the relaxation of this regulation.

Unfortunately, much of the legislation with which designers must work appears to be based on the pattern illustrated by the daylighting example. Wherever there is the possibility of measuring performance, there is also the opportunity to legislate. It is difficult to legislate for qualities, but easy to define and enforce quantities. It is increasingly difficult for the designer to maintain a sensibly balanced design process in the face of necessarily imbalanced legislation. One of the most heavily legislated design problems today is to be found in public sector housing. Apart from the building regulations, some of which are especially demanding in the case of housing, the architect has to observe the government mandatory minimum standards for local authority housing. Many of these requirements were drawn out of the 1961 Parker Morris research report on "Homes for Today and Tomorrow". It is interesting to see which of the research committees many recommendations actually became mandatory requirements and which did not. Consider three of the original Parker Morris recommendations about kitchens.

1. The relation of the kitchen to the place outside the kitchen where the children are likely to play should be considered.
2. A person working at the sink should be able to see out of the window.
3. Worktops should be provided on both sides of the sink and cooker positions. Kitchen fitments should be arranged to form a work sequence comprising worktop/sink/worktop/cooker/worktop unbroken by a door or any other traffic way.

All these recommendations seem sensible and desirable. As criteria of performance however they are not all so easily measured from an architect's drawing. In fact only the last recommendation became a mandatory requirement. Thus it is now quite permissible to design a family maisonette or flat off the ground with no view of any outside play spaces from the kitchen, but with the very model of a kitchen work surface as may not be found even in some very expensive privately built housing. It is worth noting that this legislation was introduced during the early period of what has now been called first generation design methodology. Reference has already been made to Alexander's (1964) famous method of design, which perhaps exemplifies the thinking about design at this time, and we shall pause here to fill in some detail.

Alexander's method involved first listing all the requirements of a particular design problem, and then looking for interactions between these requirements. For example in the design of a kettle some requirements for the choice of materials might be as follows.

Simplicity: the fewer the materials the more efficient the factory

Performance: each function within the kettle requires its own material e.g. handle, lid, spout

Jointing: the fewer the materials the less and the simpler the jointing and the less the maintenance

Economy: choose the cheapest material suitable

The interactions between each pair of these requirements are next labelled as positive, negative or neutral depending on whether they complement, inhibit or have no effect upon each other. In this case all the interactions except jointing/simplicity are negative since they show conflicting requirements. For example while the performance requirement suggests many materials, the jointing and simplicity

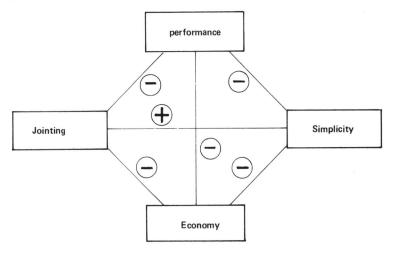

5.7 The requirements and their interactions for "Alexander's kettle"

requirements would ideally be satisfied by using only one material. Thus jointing and simplicity interact positively with each other but both interact negatively with performance. Thus a designer using Alexander's method would first list all the requirements of his design and then state which pairs of requirements interact either positively or negatively. All this data would then be fed into a computer program which looks for clusters of requirements which are heavily inter-related but relatively unconnected with other requirements. The computer would then print out these clusters effectively breaking the problem down into independent sub-problems each relatively simple for the designer to understand and solve.

Alexander's work has been heavily criticised, not least by himself, (Alexander 1966) and an excellent review of many of its failings is to be found in Broadbent's book *Design in Architecture* (1973). Some of Alexander's most obvious errors, and those which interest us here, result from a rather mechanistic view of the nature of design problems which is enshrined in much housing legislation which is still in force today. Alexander summarises his attitudes towards design problems as "the problem is defined by a set of requirements called M. The solution to this problem will be a form which successfully satisfies all of these requirements." Implicit in this statement are a number of notions now commonly rejected (Lawson 1979). First, that there exists a set of requirements which can be exhaustively listed at the start of the design process. As we saw in chapter 3, this is not really feasible since all sorts of requirements are quite likely to occur to designer and client alike

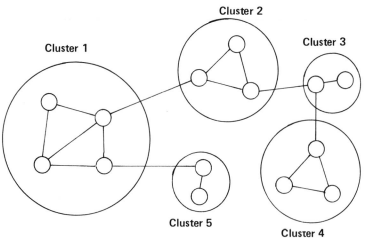

5.8 Alexander's method sought to identify clusters of relatively independent requirements which could be considered separately

even well after the synthesis of solutions has started. The second misconception in Alexander's method is that all these listed requirements are of equal value and that the interactions between them are all equally strong. Common sense would suggest that it is quite likely to be much more important to satisfy some requirements than others, and that some pairs of requirements may be closely related while others are more loosely connected. Third, and rather more subtly Alexander fails to appreciate that some requirements and interactions have much more profound implications for the form of the solution than do others.

To illustrate these deficiencies consider two pairs of interacting requirements listed by Chermayeff and Alexander (1963) in their study of community and privacy in housing design. The first interaction is between "efficient parking for owners and visitors; adequate manoeuvre space" and "separation of children and pets from vehicles". The second interaction is between "stops against crawling and climbing insects, vermin, reptiles, birds and mammals" and "filters against smells, viruses, bacteria, dirt. Screens against flying insects, wind-blown dust, litter, soot and garbage." The trouble with Alexander's method is that it is incapable of distinguishing between these interactions in terms of strength, quality or importance, and yet any experienced architect would realise that the two problems have quite different kinds of solution implications. The first is a matter of access and thus poses a spatial planning problem while the second raises an issue about the detailed technical design of the building skin. In a normal design process these two problems would be given emphasis at quite different stages. Thus in this sense the designer selects the aspects of the problem he wishes to consider in order of their likely impact on the solution as a whole. In this case, issues of general layout and organisation would come long before the detailing of doors and windows. Unfortunately the cluster pattern generated by Alexander's method conceals this natural meaning in the problem and forces a strange way of working on the designer.

The rather bald, value-free list of requirements which is the central feature of Alexander's method bears a strikingly close resemblance to the Parker Morris report and subsequent Government Mandatory Minimum Standards for Local Authority Housing. Because the solution implications of these mandatory requirements are so specific it is easy for the designer to find himself designing literally from the kitchen sink, and worktops, outwards. When a requirement is mandatory it has no relative value, just as in Alexander's method, and must be satisfied whatever the sacrifices. Designers working with such legislation must be careful not to act like the student who, when sitting an examination, tends to answer the compulsory question first.

Such design legislation has only recently come under close and critical scrutiny, and designers have begun to report the failings of legislation in practice. In 1973 the Essex County Council produced its now classic Design Guide for Residential Areas, which was an attempt to deal with both qualitative and quantitative aspects of housing design. Visual standards and such concepts as privacy were given as much emphasis as noise levels or efficient traffic circulation. Whilst the objectives of this and the many other design guides which followed were almost universally applauded, many designers have recently expressed concern at the results of such notes for guidance actually being used in practice as legislation. The national building regulations have come under increasing criticism from architects who have shown how they often create undesirable results (Lawson 1975) and proposals are now being put forward to revise the whole system of building control (Savidge 1978).

In 1976 the Department of the Environment published its research report no 6 on the Value of Standards for the External Residential Environment which concluded that many currently accepted standards were either unworkable or even positively objectionable. The report firmly rejected the imposition of requirements for such matters as privacy, view, sunlight or daylight. "The application of standards across the board defeats the aim of appropriately different provision in different situations." This report seems to sound the final death knell for legislation based on the 1960's first generation design methodology. "The qualities of good design are not encapsulated in quantitative standards ... It is right for development controllers to ask that adequate provision be made for, say, privacy or access or children's play or quiet. The imposition of specified quantities as requirements is a different matter, and is not justified by design results."

Perhaps it is because design problems are often so intractable and nebulous that the temptation is so great to seek out measurable criteria of satisfactory performance. The difficulty for the designer here is to place value on such criteria and thus balance them against each other and factors which cannot be quantitatively measured. Regrettably numbers seem to confer respectability and importance on what might actually be quite trivial factors. Boje (1971) in his book on open-plan office design provides us with an excellent demonstration of this numerical measuring disease. He calculates that it takes on average about 7 seconds to open and close an office door. Put this together with some research which shows that in an office building accommodating 100 people in 25 rooms on average each person will change rooms some 11 times in a day and thus, in an open plan office Boje argues, each person would save some 32 door movements or 224 seconds per working day. Using similar logic Boje calculates the increased working efficiency resulting from the optimal arrangements of heating, lighting and telephones. From all this Boje is then able to conclude that a properly designed open-plan office will save some 2,000 minutes per month per employee over a conventional design.

The unthinking designer could easily use such apparently high quality and convincing data to design an office based on such factors as minimising "person door movements". But in fact such figures are quite useless unless the designer also knows just how relatively important it is to save 7 seconds of time. Would that 7 seconds saved actually be used productively? What other, perhaps more critical, social and interpersonal effects result from the lack of doors and walls? So many more questions need answering before the simple single index of "person door movements" can become of value in a design context.

Because in design there are often so many variables which cannot be measured on the same scale value judgements seem inescapable. For example in designing electrical power tools convenience of use has often to be balanced against safety, or portability against robustness. Although it may prove possible to measure designs on crude scales of satisfaction for each of these factors, they remain difficult to relate. Thus a very lightweight lawn mower while being easy to manoeuvre and push might also prove to be noisy and easily damaged. For such an item there is no one right answer since different purchasers are likely to place different values on factors such as manoeuvrability or reliability. The sensible manufacturer of such equipment will produce a whole range of alternative designs each offering different advantages and disadvantages. The problem of relative values however becomes much more critical when design decisions are being taken for large numbers of people who may not have the choice available to the purchasers of new lawn mowers. Examples of such design problems include public sector housing or a new school, the routing of new roads or the siting of factories. Inherently, such projects involve varying degrees of benefit to some and losses to others. A new motorway may well save a long distance motorist's time and relieve congestion in nearby towns while subjecting local residents to noise and pollution.

Attempts have been made to apply cost-benefit analysis techniques to

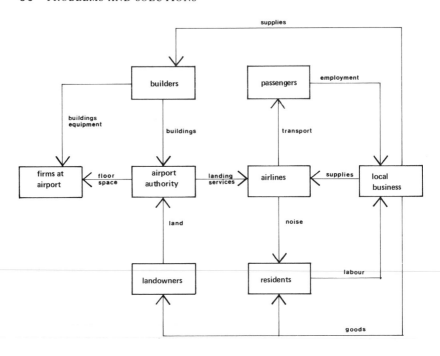

5.9   A simplified diagram of some of the effects various interested parties have on each other when a new airport is built

these kinds of design problem. Cost-benefit analysis relies upon expressing all factors in terms of their monetary value, thus establishing a common metric. Unfortunately, some factors are rather more easily costed than others. This is perhaps best illustrated by reference to one of the most well known applications of cost-benefit analysis, the Roskill Commission on the siting of the third London airport. After a number of preliminary stages during which some seventy-eight sites were considered the commission narrowed the choice down to four sites at Cublington, Foulness, Nuthampstead and Thurleigh which were then compared using cost-benefit analysis. Even the grossly simplified diagram reproduced here gives some idea of the complex array of effects which the various interested parties could be expected to have on each other as a result of such a project. In fact there are many other much wider effects not shown which include such matters as the distortion of the national transportation network resulting from the provision of new forms of access to the chosen site. For example the opening of an airport at Cublington would have resulted in the closure of the existing Luton airport which would have been too close for air traffic control procedures.

Many of the benefits of the airport in terms of the profits to the various transportation authorities and other companies were reasonably easy to calculate for each site and could be set against the profits lost from the existing use of land. The costs of providing the access transportation to each site and the costs in terms of journey time were also fed into the equation. Losses in terms of reduced amenity however proved more difficult to assess in purely monetary terms. These effects range from otherwise unwanted expenditure resulting from people having to leave their homes, through such factors as the depreciation in value of property in the surrounding area to the noise annoyance caused by the operation of the airport. Such a public use of cost-benefit analysis revealed many of the real dangers involved in basing decisions on the quantification of qualitative factors such as the amenity of an environment. Obviously the success of such a process is contingent upon the assumption that all the costs of amenity loss have been correctly valued. The real difficulty here is that such valuations are unlikely to be arrived at by consensus in a pluralistic society. The costing of noise annoyance or the value of quiet had proved difficult enough for the Roskill Commission, but when considerations of the conservation of wildlife at Foulness were introduced to the argument the whole decision making process began to split at the seams. Cost-benefit analysis was clearly incapable of developing one equation to balance the profits of an airport against the loss of a totally unproductive but irreplacable and, some would say, priceless sanctuary for birdlife. The Roskill report itself recognised the futility of attempting totally objective judgement in comparing the Cublington and Foulness sites. The choice was between the damage to the value of Aylesbury and the loss of a fine Norman church at Stewkley or the ruining of the Essex coastline and probable extinction of the dark-bellied Brent goose.

As with much else in this inquiry there is no single right answer however much each individual may believe there is. For us to claim to judge absolutely between these views (the importance of conservation of buildings or wildlife) is to claim gifts of wisdom and prophecy which no man can possess. All we can do is respect both points of view. (Roskill Commission Report).

Even the costings of the more ostensibly easily quantifiable factors proved extremely debatable. For example the cost-benefit research team itself revised the assumptions on which total construction costs had been based. This change proved so drastic that Cublington moved from being the most costly to the least costly of the few sites in this respect. As the inquiry proceeded it gradually became apparent that many of the fundamental underlying assumptions necessary for the cost-benefit analysis could similarly be challenged. Basing the whole decision making process on arguments developed from such questionable assumptions proved too uncomfortable for at least one member of the commission. In his minority report Professor Buchanan described how "I became more and more anxious lest I be trapped in a process which I did not fully understand and ultimately led without choice to a conclusion which I would know in my heart of hearts I did not agree with."

In the final analysis it seems unreasonable for designers to expect to find a process which will protect them from the painful and difficult business of exercising subjective judgement in situations where both quantitative and qualitative factors must be taken into account. The attempt to reduce all factors to a common quantitative measure such as monetary value frequently serves only to shift the problem to one of valuation. The Roskill Commission on the siting of the third London airport provided one further lesson of importance here. Designers and those who make design-like decisions which profoundly affect the lives of many people can no longer expect their value judgements to be made in private. Such large-scale design processes must clearly invite the participation of all those who will be substantially affected. How that participation should be organised is another matter beyond the scope of this particular book.

6 A model of design problems

As an artist I did not set out to make the public understand but to find problems for myself of space and form, and to explore them.

Henry Moore (on his 80th birthday)

Open-ended problems are both easy and difficult to solve. They are easy in that even untutored persons can arrive at a solution, but difficult when the solver sets forth a comprehensive list of criteria to which his solution must conform and, whether implicitly or explicitly he attends to this list in his solution.

Robert Wehrli, Open-ended Problem Solving in Design

The generators of design problems

It is sometimes difficult to separate design from art. The products of design are frequently seen by the public as artistic, even sometimes actually as "works of art", and designers themselves are indeed also often artists. Even the drawings generated by designers to illustrate their schemes can sometimes easily be confused with works of art. Whether or not an object can rightly be described as a "work of art" is a matter which lies beyond the scope of this book. What is of importance here is not the product but the process. The creative process which may give rise to a work of art undoubtedly shares much in common with the design process, and many of the same talents may be needed for both. What is usually different however is the nature of the source of the problem. Perhaps it is only a difference of degree, but nevertheless the difference is real enough and of fundamental significance in determining the nature of the processes of art and design. While the artist may sometimes be commissioned to produce work for a particular place or occasion he is more often entirely his own master. The artist deals with issues and solves problems which seem important to him. The artist may respond to his own work and is free to shift his attention and change the problem to one which fascinates him more. Such artistic problems are rarely clearly articulated by the artist outside his work. It is usually critics and historians who retrospectively interpret and identify

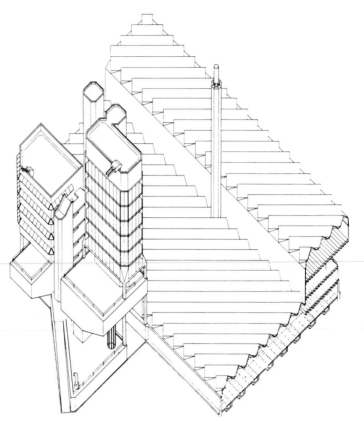

6.1 It is sometimes difficult to tell, as with this drawing by the architect James Stirling for the project for the Leicester University Engineering Department (1959) by James Stirling and James Gowan, whether we are looking at a design drawing or a "work of art"

the issues which appear to them to have been uppermost in the artist's mind. When asked by a music critic to explain one of his operas, Wagner is reported to have responded rather testily "but it is the explanation." The artist largely generates his own tasks, and although he may struggle, perhaps for some considerable time, to solve these problems he may never fully articulate them other than through his art itself.

In this respect the designer is faced with a different situation altogether. In design, the problem usually originates not in the designer's mind but with a client or user; someone in need who is unable to solve the problem, or perhaps, even fully to understand it without help. The designer, unlike the artist, is almost always commissioned; the task, albeit ill-defined, is brought to him. But the designer himself is often expected to contribute problems too. In this sense he is assumed by his client to be artistic and his role is at least partly interpretive. An architect's client expects rather more than just a house with rooms of appropriate sizes and relationships. He expects that, in addition to the problems that he lays before the architect, other issues of form, space and style will be considered. This client–designer relationship works both ways, for the architect also expects to be given some freedom in the definition of the design problem. It is even quite likely that the designer receiving a new commission is looking forward to being able further to explore problems in which he is already interested. The extent to which the designer is allowed this artistic self-gratification is a function both of the nature of the problem and of the client–designer relationship. For this reason there is perhaps inherently an element of tension in the client–designer relationship. Both are dependent one upon the other and yet both in their different ways are anxious of the other exerting too much control. The designer while needing his fee realises that his reputation is largely the result of his past work and is thus anxious to continue developing his ideas through solutions for all to see. The client on the other hand cannot actually design by himself but nevertheless may to some extent know what he wants and is anxious lest the designer get quite different ideas. Obviously the wise client chooses a designer who, on the basis of his past work, looks likely to share an interest in the client's problems. No-one could have ever expected Mies van der Rohe and Edwin Lutyens to have designed even remotely similar houses for the same client on the same site: as architects their own personal interests were too different.

It is worth noting at this point that the distinction between art and design is, like all such man-made conceptual boundaries, rather hazy and easily blurred. Students, groping to establish their role as designers are often confused by work which defies easy classification. When Peter Cook produced his highly influential "Plug-in-City" in 1964 it at first appeared to be a piece of design; a city, admittedly imaginary and of the future, but nevertheless which looked like architecture and many of the drawings were themselves very architectural. In fact the process and intention behind such work is in some ways more akin to the artistic than the design process. "Plug-in-City" did not solve any immediate problems, nor was it intended to be built. Rather it explored and expressed ideas, beliefs and values, and asked provocative questions about the future direction of city design and patterns of life. It is entirely appropriate that design students should be interested in, and influenced by such work, just as they might be by poetry, prose, paintings or films

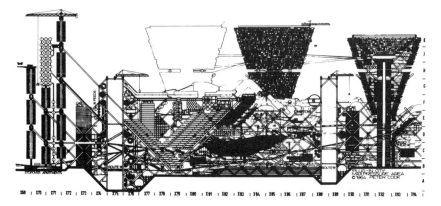

6.2 This drawing by Peter Cook of his *Plug-in-city* is more like visual propaganda than a conventional design drawing

about similar issues. But they should not expect to approach real-world design problems posed by clients in the more introspective and personally expressive mode of the artist. Designers, unlike artists, cannot devote themselves exclusively to problems which are of interest to themselves personally.

The relationship between client and designer itself actually constitutes part of the design problem. The way that designers perceive and understand problems is to some extent a function of this social relationship. Such issues are scarcely mentioned in many books on design methodology, where design problems are apparently expected to materialise as if handed down on stone tablets. The vast majority of design today is commissioned by clients who are not themselves the users. Public architecture such as hospitals, schools or housing is usually designed by publicly-employed architects who have relatively little contact with the users of their buildings. At the other end of the scale industrial design and graphic design are directed at a mass market and are usually commissioned by commercial clients. The traditional image of the designer establishing a personal relationship with a client/ user is grossly misleading. Even private practitioner architects commissioned to design new buildings for large organisations such as universities are likely to be buffered from the actual users by a client committee or even a full-time buildings department. Frequently communication between designers and their users is both indirect and, as Page (1972) has argued, filtered by organisational politics. In his study of "planning and protest" Page describes the "people barriers" erected in many organisations to prevent too much disruptive user feedback reaching designers. In local authorities for example both the politicians and administrators may attempt to establish themselves as the communication channel between the designers and the users outside in order to force through policy or maintain a powerful position in the system. On balance such organisational barriers, whatever advantages they give to the client body in terms of increased control over the designer, serve only to make the designer's task of understanding the problem more difficult. As many young designers must have found on leaving design schools, it is one thing to design for yourself but quite another to design for a real client with real prejudices and biases. When that client is not even the prospective user of the design the problem becomes even more remote. This increasing remoteness of designers from those for whom they design has created the need for user-requirement studies. Almost in desperation designers have turned to social and human scientists from ergonomists through architectural psychologists to urban sociologists to tell them what their users actually need. By and large this liaison between design and social science has not been as practically useful as was first hoped. Social science remains largely descriptive while design is necessarily prescriptive, so the psychologists and sociologists have gone on researching and the designers designing, and they are yet to re-educate each other into more genuinely collaborative roles. Meanwhile the communication between the creators and users of environments often remains uncomfortably remote. More recently attempts have been made to involve users more in the design process, and a discussion of some of these participatory techniques will follow in chapter 13.

So far we have seen how design problems whilst usually initiated by a client may be contributed to by both users and designers themselves. Finally we must briefly turn our attention to another generator of design problems, perhaps the most remote of all from the designer, the legislator. Although frequently not involved in the actual design itself legislators create constraints within which designers must work. Such legislation and control may range from standards and codes of practice to guidelines and recommendations. Such standards may govern factors of safety, utility or appearance. They may have to be satisfied in order to sell products on the market, to allow conventional trade descriptions or to permit building construction to commence. Design legislation today may cover anything from the safety of electrical goods to the honesty of advertising or the energy consumption of buildings. In many cases complete bureaucracies exist to administer and interpret this general legislation for each specific instance. The architect today must satisfy the fire officer, the building inspector and the town planner and in addition,

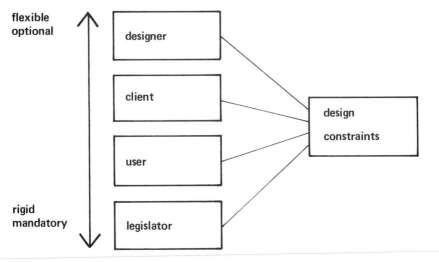

6.3 The generators of design constraints

depending on the nature of the particular project, the housing corporation, health inspectors, Home Office inspectors, the water authority, electricity authority, the Post Office, factory inspectors and so the list goes on.

As we have seen, legislative constraints in design are generally value-free. That is to say they must be satisfied without question, and cannot be weighed against other factors and considerations. Each of the generators of design problems identified here impose constraints upon the design solution but with different degrees of rigidity. The most rigid being those imposed by legislators and the most flexible those generated by the designer himself. For example in designing the layout for a shop interior, constraints will be imposed by each generator. In order to ensure safety in case of fire the fire officer will require the surface materials to achieve a specified rate of resistance to flame spread, he will determine the number and position of escape doors and the width of corridors and gangways. Other legislation may control the display and storage of food, the working conditions of staff and so on. The client too will generate many design constraints connected with the primary objectives of attracting custom and selling goods. Unlike the legislator's constraints the designer is able to discuss the client's constraints and establish priorities. When he discovers apparent conflicts between the design implications of the client's objectives the designer is able to go back to his client and jointly they may re-appraise the client constraints. For example on the one hand the client for our shop may want the display furniture to be designed and arranged so as to make the goods look attractive and to tempt prospective purchasers. On the other hand he will certainly wish to minimise the likelihood of shoplifting or damage to unbought items. These two requirements are at least to some extent in conflict. In Alexander's terms they interact negatively. However the exact balance of satisfaction for such requirements may not be clear to the client until the designer explores the various possibilities in physical, three-dimensional, terms. He may not be able to say exactly what degree of risk of loss from theft he is prepared to tolerate to achieve effectiveness of display until the designer actually shows him some drawings or models.

Clearly from the designer's point of view client constraints are not absolute as are legislator constraints. Rather they all carry a relative value which is open to a certain amount of discussion. In this example the designer too is expected to generate his own constraints. He is supposed to come up with an integrative idea, an overall concept which organises and unifies the whole shop. The constraints he generates may restrict the range of colours and materials and establish geometric and dimensional rules. The goods for sale in the shop may range from items as small as buttons through books and stationery to clothes and furniture. The shopfittings must be capable of displaying all these goods and perhaps establish a distinct but related image for each department. One idea might be to devise a range of fittings constructed of bent plywood covered in brightly-coloured laminates combined with curved chromium plated tubular frames. Having established the constraint of these materials and forms the designer would have to create actual fittings for clothes, food, jewellery and so on.

It is obvious that these designer-generated constraints are comparatively flexible. If they cause too many difficulties, or just simply do not work out the designer is free to modify or scrap them altogether. Design students often fail to recognise this simple fact but instead continue to pit their wits endlessly and fruitlessly against insuperable problems which are largely of their own making. One of the most important skills a designer must acquire is the ability critically to evaluate his own self-imposed constraints and we shall return to this again in a later chapter on design strategies. For the time being it is important to recognise the different contributions to the problem made by each of the major generators of constraints.

The domain of design constraints

Constraints in design result largely from required or desired relationships between two or more elements. For example, in housing

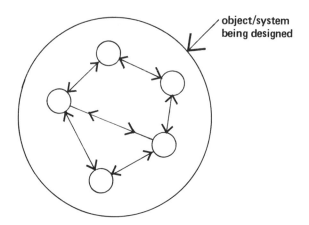

6.4   Internal constraints are imposed by the relationships desired between parts of the object or system being designed

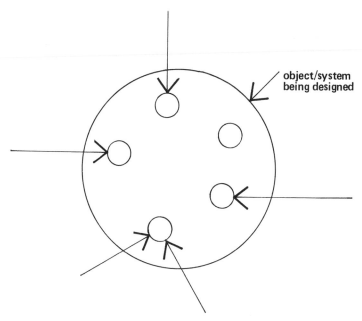

6.5   External constraints are imposed when a relationship is desired with something which exists outside the object or system being designed

the legislator demands that there is a worktop on either side of the cooker, the client might express a wish for both the kitchen and living room to open directly onto the dining room and the architect may think it sensible to try to organise all the spaces around a central structural and service core. As we have seen the legislator's demand is fixed, the

GENERATOR

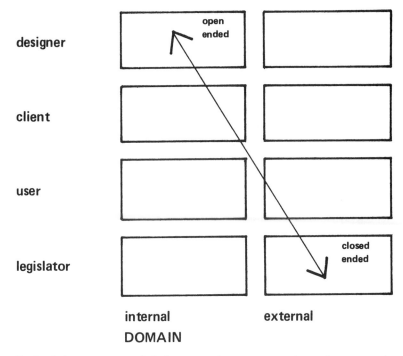

6.6 Each of the generators of design constraints can create internal or external constraints. Each box in the diagram poses its own special kind of problem

client may alter his priorities as the design implications unfold and the designer may change his mind altogether. What links all the constraints in this example is their domain of influence. All establish relationships between elements of the object being designed, in this case a house. They are entirely internal to the problem and we shall therefore call them internal constraints. Consider by contrast the following equally hypothetical, but quite likely, set of constraints. The building regulations closely define the permitted distances of windows from boundaries so as to avoid the risk of a fire spreading to adjacent properties. The client may have a strong preference for a living room which overlooks the garden and has a sunny aspect. The architect may think it important to continue the existing street facade in terms of line and height. Here the constraints establish a relationship between some element of the house and some feature of its site. They relate the designed object to its context, and in each case one end of the relationship, the site boundary, the sun, the street, is external to the problem. We shall therefore refer to these as external constraints. At this point it is worth noting from the examples used to illustrate these constraints that both internal and external constraints may be generated by designers, clients and legislators. So far the model of design constraints appears two dimensional, the dimensions being the generator and the domain of constraints.

The essential significance of the domain of a constraint lies in the freedom available to the designer. Internal constraints generally allow a greater degree of freedom and choice since they only govern factors which are under the designer's control. To return to the housing example, in achieving the client's desired relationship between kitchen and dining room the designer is able to position both. External constraints are not so simple. The client's wish to have a sunny living room is in a sense a more demanding requirement, because much though he might like to the architect cannot control the movements of the sun! For this reason external constraints, although they may sometimes only constitute a small part of the total problem are often highly significant. Such factors as the site, location, or the specific context in which a design is to be used all create external constraints which emphasise the individual and particular nature of the design.

For the fashion designer external constraints range from the manufacturing process, whether it be hand-made or mass produced, to the human body itself. Off the peg clothes are obviously designed around average bodily dimensions but for the one-off high fashion designer the external constraints of a particular shape, personality and occasion provide the inspiration for the design of unique garments intended to be worn in one specific context.

In theatre design, neither the play nor the stage are under the control of the designer, but a particular combination of the two might inspire him to produce a unique set. The dramatic demands of the play together with the visual and acoustic properties and problems of the stage comprise a highly significant collection of constraints. Sometimes external constraints virtually determine the whole form of design. What makes one bridge different from another are the site conditions, the span needed, and the position and quality of supporting ground. The Severin Bridge across the Rhine at Cologne is supported by taut cables fanning out from the top of a single A shaped frame sited on conveniently accessible supporting ground about a third of the way across the river. The conventional two tower suspension structure would have seriously obscured the down river view of the massively

6.7 The unusual Severin Bridge across the Rhine at Cologne owes its form to external constraints

impressive cathedral which dominates the skyline. Here the unusual site conditions, combined with the architect's concern not to disturb the Cologne skyline, have resulted in an extraordinarily distinguished and fresh solution to an age-old problem of civil engineering.

6.8   The architect's drawings for the Severin Bridge showing how the single tower preserves the view of Cologne Cathedral

External constraints can be just as influential and inspirational at the other end of the spectrum of design. Paul Rand (1970) in his classical book on graphic design explains how what he calls "the given material" forms an important starting point in advertising graphics. Rand's "given materials" are in essence the external constraints of graphic design. The product to be promoted, the format and medium of the advertisement and the production process itself. Such factors are not under the designer's control, like the movement of the sun they already exist and he must relate his work to them.

The role of internal constraints in the design process is probably sufficiently obvious to need little elaboration here. For an architect the internal constraints frequently comprise the majority of his brief. The number and sizes of spaces of various kinds and qualities form the most obvious client-generated internal constraints. The structure or pattern of the problem for the architect lies in the desired relationships between these spaces. These relationships may be in terms of human circulation and the distribution of services, or in the visual and acoustic connections and barriers necessary to house the various communal and private functions of the building. Architects conventionally begin to grapple with these internal constraints very early on in the process by drawing bubble diagrams and flow charts which graphically represent the required relationships.

One of the most fascinating features of the design process for its would-be students seems to be the nature of the role played by external and internal constraints in the designer's mind. Clearly the balance of importance is not always the same. Perhaps one of the reasons why students of architecture find housing design so difficult is because the balance of external and internal constraints is very even. Unlike many other buildings the architect may design, the house has an internal structure which is relatively simple and easily understood. What makes the internal planning of an individual house difficult however is the problem of relating it to adjacent houses and other features of the site. The indications are that the experienced housing architect will use a process quite unlike that employed by the novice student. Before tackling housing for the first time the student is quite likely to have designed such buildings as schools or offices, where the internal planning was of paramount importance. So he has begun to develop a design process based on exploring internal constraints and thus may initially turn his attention to the house itself. By contrast the experienced housing architect already has a good grasp of the basic variations of house planning and is much more likely to concentrate on the site. In her study of the design of six housing estates in London Darke (1978) quotes several of the architects explaining their design process in just this way. Douglas Stephen was perhaps the most explicit: "I don't think of house plans at all at the beginning ... I think entirely of the site and of the restrictions, and there are not only spatial restrictions but also social restrictions on the site." Other architects were less practical and more romantic about the influences of the site. Kate Macintosh thought that "you should try to express the unique quality of the site" and Michael Neylan confirmed that "we try to get the building to respond and breathe with its surroundings." All these architects are experienced and distinguished designers of housing and this response to a new problem is quite understandable when one remembers that the problems of a house remain fairly constant but each site is unique. As Neyland puts it: "the whole point of good housing is the relationship between the unit (house) and what's around it." Perhaps it is this very close and critical interplay between internal and external constraints which makes housing such a fascinating but difficult design problem. It certainly seems likely that the balance of internal and external constraints in a design problem is of considerable significance in determining the nature of that problem and the designer's response to it. We shall return to this point again in the next section in a discussion of design strategies.

The function of design constraints

We have seen how design problems are built up of constraints which may be either entirely internal to the system or object being designed, or may be linked with some external factor not under the designers control. These constraints may be imposed most obviously by the client or users but also by legislators and the designer himself. The question which remains is, why are these constraints imposed? What do they achieve, what is their purpose and function? In particular here can we identify and separate different types of function and study their effect on the design process?

The purpose of constraints is obviously to ensure that the designed system or object performs the functions demanded of it as adequately as possible. For this reason it is easier to develop models of the function of constraints for specific design fields such as architecture or industrial design. Hillier and Leaman (1972) have proposed such a model intended to help organise research in architecture. According to this model, buildings can be seen to perform four functions, modifying climate, behaviour, resources and culture. Hillier and Leaman claim that "buildings have tended to be over designed from the point of view of the relation between activity and its spatial containment, just as they have been under-designed from the point of view of climate modification". This model has thus been used to argue for a redirection of attention in architectural research and a shift of emphasis in design. The model has been useful in exposing the argument about which functions should be allowed to dominate in the design process and why. Markus (1969) provides another example of such function models used for research in specific areas. His Building Performance Research Unit also used a four function model in appraising the performance of buildings. Markus sees the functions of buildings as divided between: the building system of physical components, the environmental system which is similar to Hillier and Leaman's climate modifying function, the activity/behaviour system which is again similar to Hillier and Leaman, and finally the organisational system which the building houses. Perhaps because of their very practical emphasis Markus' team failed to see buildings as contributing more widely to culture or even as symbolic entities. Markus considers the cost system not to be independent as do Hillier and Leaman but rather prefers to see cost, or resource, implications of achieving each of the other four groups of objectives.

Rand (1970) stresses the importance of both form and content in graphic design. The commercial designer is charged with communicating a message through a piece of two-dimensional design. Clearly then his work has a central symbolic and communicative function, but it is also important for the message, which itself might be quite ordinary, to be striking, unusual, demanding of attention and memorable. The graphic designer deals in two-dimensional composition using colour, texture, form, contrast, proportion, line, shape and so on. The manipulation of these formal materials add style and character to the message, making it recognisable.

These two functions of form and content are obviously the essence of graphic design but they are also important in any of the environmental design fields. Whatever the designer's intentions might be we inevitably perceive his work on these two levels of the formal and the symbolic. The Union Jack is not just a pattern of colour and form but it is also inescapably a national symbol. Some buildings, like cathedrals have very powerful symbolic functions while others, such as houses may have less dramatic but possibly just as important a symbolic purpose.

There are many more models of the functions of design constraints in specific contexts which we could review and most of them have at least some useful features. However for the purposes of this more general

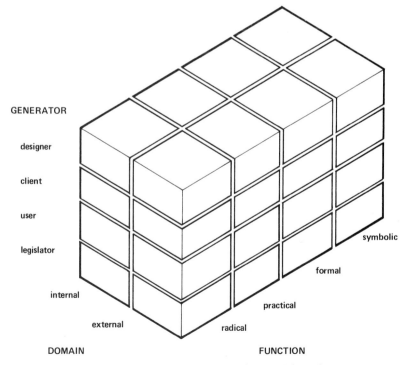

6.9 The completed model of design constraints (repeated for reference on page 202)

6.10 The architect Denys Lasdun intended the horizontal platforms of the National Theatre to solve radical, formal and symbolic problems

model we will adopt four functions, which in addition to formal and symbolic include radical and practical. While these four functions are fairly exhaustive some readers may like to add others or subdivide some to suit more specialised fields of design.

The radical constraints are those which deal with the primary purpose of the object or system being designed. "Radical" is used here not in the sense of revolutionary or left wing but in its true meaning of fundamental. Thus in the design of a school the radical constraints are those to do with the educational system itself.

The practical constraints are those aspects of the total design problem which deal with the reality of producing, making or building the design; the technological problem. For the architect such problems include the external factors of the bearing capacity of site and the internal factors of the materials used in construction. For the graphic designer there are the practical problems of printing and reprographic technology and the media of transmission.

The completed model of design problems now shows how in theory each of the generators may contribute each type of constraint. In practice, however, each tends to generate rather more of one type than another. Thus the client/user is responsible for the majority of the radical constraints and is likely to contribute some symbolic ones, while the designer is the main generator of the formal and the practical and also contributes symbolic constraints. More importantly, it is the designer's task to integrate and co-ordinate all these constraints by whatever device he can. We shall see more of this process in the next section but an interesting example from the work of Denys Lasdun will serve to illustrate the point here. In his account of the National Theatre Lasdun (1976) explains how the horizontal platforms, which he calls strata, and which form such a dominant element throughout the building serve as such an integrating device solving radical, formal and symbolic problems.

They support the interior functions while allowing for flexible planning. They provide coherence to a large scheme which is, nonetheless, broken down to the human scale. They give visual expression to the essentially public nature of the institution: for a theatre must be a place where human contact is enriched and a common experience is shared.

The use of the model

It is important to recognise that this is a model not of the design process (like those reviewed in chapter 3) but rather of design problems. In the next section we shall see something of the way the process can be charted as the designer shifts his attention from one part of the problem to another or the way in which he explores relationships between parts of the problem. This model is not intended to form part of a design method but rather as an aid to the understanding of the nature of design problems, and thus only indirectly to assist in establishing a design process.

This book began with a question. How is it that we can still use the word design to describe such different processes as the creation of motor cars, architecture or advertisements? Reference to the model will show that such situations differ only in the degree of importance attached to various aspects of the problem. We expect that a fashion designer will lay great emphasis on designer-generated formal and symbolic constraints. Architects are expected to take more notice of their clients and users and, because architecture is so public a matter, to respect legislative controls. Sometimes internal constraints will be dominant and sometimes the design may be largely formed by external factors.

Design situations can be seen to vary in terms of the overall degree of freedom and control available to the designer. Where the bulk of the constraints are internal and designer-generated we talk of open-ended design. Where, by contrast, clients or legislators make heavy demands or there are many external factors to consider we talk of tightly constrained design. Some designers seem to prefer the open-ended situation while others are more at home with tighter problems. Recognising the nature of the problem and responding with an appropriate design process seems to be one of the most important skills in design. It is very easy to neglect a set of constraints. Modern architects are often criticised for their lack of attention to the symbolic functions of design and for producing architecture which seems aggressive or inhuman. Students of design often devote too much of their time to unimportant parts of the problem. It is easy for the inexperienced to generate almost impossible practical problems by slavishly following ill-conceived formal ideas which remain unquestioned but could quite easily be modified. One of the major roles of design tutors is to move their students around from one part of the problem to another and the job of the design student is to learn to do it for himself.

7 Problems and solutions

Men have become like gods. Isn't it about time that we understood our divinity? Science offers us total mastery over our environment and over our destiny, yet instead of rejoicing we feel deeply afraid. Why should this be? How might these fears be resolved?

Edmund Leach, 1967 Reith Lectures

We look at the present through a rear-view mirror. We march backwards into the future. Suburbia lives imaginatively in Bonanza-land.

Marshall McLuhan, *The Medium is the Message*

Now and when

The designer is primarily helping to create a future world, and in this sense his task is inevitably confounded by many doubts and uncertainties. How well will his work be received by clients and users and will it really satisfy their needs? How well will it sell and how long will it last? These crucial questions can only be answered by the passage of time and the designer, having completed his work can only subject it to the test of time and wait patiently for the verdict. Such doubts and worries must have plagued the minds of many generations of designers, but now there are new and even more unsettling uncertainties facing contemporary designers.

The advanced technocratic society for which today's designer works is itself changing rapidly. Unlike previous generations we live in a world with comparatively little tradition and cultural stability. The vast majority of our everyday environment has been designed and even invented within our own generation. The motor car and the television profoundly influence our daily lives to an extent that would probably have astonished their inventors, and the laser and the computer now seem likely to have just as widespread an influence on our future. Many writers have tried to explore the consequences of such rapid and dramatic change. Marshall McLuhan (1967) comments on the importance of the information explosion caused by printing, television and computers and he concludes that the only certainty in modern life is change. Dickson (1974) sees technology as the major determinant of the structure of society, and he argues that the negative societal effects of high technology suggest we should seek alternative, less harmful forms of technology. Toffler (1970) has warned that if technology continues to advance in the present manner we shall all suffer from a cultural disorientation which he calls Futureshock.

Polemical though some of these popularist writers may be there is no doubt that such rapid change does result in a world which is increasingly difficult to understand and predict, so that we are simultaneously excited and fearful about the future. Perhaps we do indeed live in what Leach (1968) calls a "Runaway world"

Men have become like gods. Isn't it about time that we understood our divinity? Science offers us total mastery over our environment and over our destiny, yet instead of rejoicing we feel deeply afraid.

Leach (1968)

All of this makes life even more difficult for the designer who is now not just uncertain how well his design will work but is even unsure of the nature of the world into which it must fit. Often in recent years we have seen the design process actually outpaced by social and technological change. The nature of medicine and attitudes towards health care have often changed too quickly for the designers and builders of new hospitals so that new buildings are out of date or too small before they are even completed. The third London airport, already discussed, has still not been built and it is by no means clear that it will now even be necessary. Developments in aircraft design and communication technology combined with rapidly changing energy costs easily outstrip the rate at which such an airport could be built. The power of the mass media can create sudden and fundamental changes of fashion and taste, leaving mass-produced items like motor cars looking outdated long before the end of their useful life.

How then can the designer respond to this uncertainty about the future? There seem to be at least three basic discernible design approaches towards such uncertain futures; procrastination, non-committal design and throw-away design. Each have their advocates and each seem to be used in identifiable situations. The first approach, procrastination, is based on the idea that somehow the future may become more certain if only we wait a little. If it is not possible to be sure of our actions now then maybe it will be easier to take a decision next year or the year after. This strategy is popular with very long

7.1 The design and building processes can easily be outpaced by changes in policy. This hospital already seemed out of date when it was opened in 1978

7.2 The short term response to an uncertain future is to build in obsolescence

timescale decision-makers such as politicians and town planners. It is on this basis that we failed to build the third London airport and that we have no clear national policy on energy supply. The real difficulty with this response to uncertainty is that once a problem has been identified it is no longer really possible to avoid the consequences of making a decision. Delaying the decision itself adds to the uncertainty and may thus accelerate the problem. Once an inner city area has been identified as in need of some planning action, that area is likely to run down or become "blighted" even more rapidly until decisions are taken about its future.

The second design response to uncertainty is to be as non-committal as possible whilst still actually proceeding. Thus architects have tended to design bland, anonymous and neutral buildings and have been accused of failing to provide sufficiently positive urban environments. A few years ago the notion of flexible and adaptable environments was popular and influential in schools of architecture. Habraken (1972) went so far as to suggest that architects should design support structures which would provide only shelter, support and services leaving future users free to create their own homes and express their own identity by arranging the kits of parts that fit within these "supports". Such ideas have remained largely theoretical and there are undoubtedly many practical and economic problems in providing buildings which are genuinely flexible and adaptable. Architects have now perhaps become slightly schizophrenic in their attitude towards flexibility. On the one hand much is said and written about designing buildings which will be able to outlast their initial function whilst on the other hand architects are increasingly finding that old buildings need not be demolished but can often easily be converted to new uses.

The third response to uncertainty is to design for the present only. Thus obsolescence is built in and the designed object is intended to be thrown away and replaced with a more up to date design. This strategy has been increasingly adopted by the designers of mass produced goods. Everything from clothes to motor cars can be discarded in favour of new styles and images. Unfortunately this consumerist approach is not only wasteful of resources but also leads to short-lived goods of continually reduced quality and thus the optional alternative of replacing outdated goods turns into a basic necessity.

Designing in times of rapid change then is clearly more difficult than designing for a stable and predictable world. As we saw in chapter 2 the rate of sociotechnic development is itself an important influence on both the design process and the role of the designer in society. But it is important to recognise that designers are not just dependent on the future, they also help to create it. Each of the design responses to uncertain futures discussed above themselves fashion the future, whether it be in the form of blighted inner city areas, indecisive architecture or out of fashion motor cars. As Jones (1970) puts it: "to design is no longer to increase the stability of the man-made world: it is to alter, for good or ill, things that determine the course of its development." In fact many of our contemporary design problems are themselves contributed to by the results of previous design activity, whether it be in the form of noise from machines or activities, or in the shape of urban decay or vandalised buildings, or in terms of dangerous and congested airports and roads. Each of these and countless other similar ailments of modern civilisation provide some of the most pressing problems facing designers, and yet to some extent at least they can "be thought of as human failures to design for conditions brought about by the products of designing" (Jones 1970).

Design problems and design solutions are inexorably interdependent. It is obviously meaningless to study solutions without reference to problems and the reverse is equally fruitless. The more one tries to isolate and study design problems the more important it becomes to refer to design solutions. In design, problems may suggest certain features of solutions but these solutions in turn create new and different problems. In chapter 3 we looked at simple definitions of design and concluded that such a complex process defied simple description. In the succeeding chapters we have explored the nature of design problems, frequently finding ourselves simultaneously involved in a discussion of solutions. It is worth pausing briefly here to summarize some of the important characteristics of design problems and solutions and the lessons that can be learnt about the nature of the design process itself. The following points should not be taken to represent a comprehensive list of discrete properties of the design situation; indeed they are often closely interrelated and there is thus some repetition. Taken together, however, they sketch an overall picture of the nature of design as it seems today.

Design problems

1 Design problems cannot be comprehensively stated

As we saw in chapter 3 one of the difficulties in developing a map of the design process is that it is never possible to be sure when all aspects of the problem have emerged. In chapter 6 we saw how design problems are generated by several groups or individuals with varying degrees of involvement in the decision making process. It is clear that many components of design problems cannot be expected to emerge until some attempt has been made at generating solutions. Indeed many features of design problems may never be fully uncovered and made explicit. Design problems are often full of uncertainties both about the objectives and their relative priorities. In fact both objectives and priorities are quite likely to change during the design process as the solution implications begin to emerge. Thus we should not expect a comprehensive and static formulation of design problems but rather they should be seen as in dynamic tension with design solutions.

2 Design problems require subjective interpretation

In the introductory first chapter we saw how designers from different fields could suggest different solutions to the same problem of what to do about railway catering not making a profit. In fact not only are designers likely to devise different solutions but they also perceive problems differently. Our understanding of design problems and the information needed to solve them depends to a certain extent upon our ideas for solving them. Thus because an industrial designer can see how to redesign the train he sees problems in the way buffet cars are laid out, while the operations researcher sees deficiences in the timetabling and scheduling of services and the graphic designer identifies inadequacies in the way the food is marketed and presented.

As we saw in chapter 5 there are many difficulties with measurement in design and problems are inevitably value-laden. In this sense design problems, like their solutions, remain a matter of subjective perception. What may seem important to one client or user or designer may not seem so to others. We should therefore not expect entirely objective formulations of design problems.

3 Design problems tend to be organised hierarchically
In chapter 4 we explored how design problems can often be viewed as symptoms of other higher-level problems illustrated by Eberhard's (1970) tale of how the problem of redesigning a doorknob was transformed into considerations of doors, walls, buildings and eventually organisations. Similarly the problem of providing an urban playground for children who roam the streets could be viewed as resulting from the design of the housing in which those children live, or the planning policy which allows vast areas of housing to be built away from natural social foci, or it could be viewed as a symptom of our educational system, or the patterns of employment of their parents. There is no objective or logical way of determining the right level on which to tackle such problems. The decision remains largely a pragmatic one; it depends on the power, time and resources available to the designer, but it does seem sensible to begin at as high a level as is reasonable and practicable.

Design solutions

1 There are an inexhaustible number of different solutions
Since design problems cannot be comprehensively stated it follows that there can never be an exhaustive list of all the possible solutions to such problems. Some of the engineering-based writers on design methodology talk of mapping out the range of possible solutions. Such a notion must obviously depend upon the assumption that the problem can be clearly and unequivocally stated, as implied by Alexander's method (see chapter 5). If however we accept the contrary viewpoint expressed here, that design problems are rather more inscrutable and ill-defined then it seems unreasonable to expect that we can be sure that all the solutions to a problem have been identified.

2 There are no optimal solutions to design problems
Design almost invariably involves compromise. Sometimes stated objectives may be in direct conflict with each other, as when motorists demand both good acceleration and low petrol consumption. Rarely can the designer simply optimise one requirement without suffering some losses elsewhere. Just how the trade-offs and compromises are made remains a matter of skilled judgement. There are thus no optimal solutions to design problems but rather a whole range of acceptable solutions (if only the designers can think of them) each likely to prove more or less satisfactory in different ways and to different clients or users. Just as the making of design decisions remains a matter of judgement so does the appraisal and evaluation of solutions. There are no established methods for deciding just how good or bad solutions are, and the best test of most design is still to wait and see how well it works in practice. Design solutions can never be perfect and are often more easily criticised than created, and designers must accept that they will almost invariably appear wrong in some ways to some people.

The Design process

1 The process is endless
Since design problems defy comprehensive description and offer an inexhaustible number of solutions the design process cannot have a finite and identifiable end. The designer's job is never really done, and he can always try to do better. In this sense designing is quite unlike puzzling. The solver of puzzles such as crosswords or mathematical problems knows when he has finished and can often recognise a correct answer, but not so the designer. The designer identifies the end of his process as a matter of judgement. It no longer seems worth the effort of going further because the chances of significantly improving on the solution seem small. This does not mean that the designer is necessarily pleased with his solution, but perhaps unsatisfactory as it might be it represents the best that he feels can be done. Time, money and information are often major limiting factors in design and a shortage of any of these essential resources can result in what the designer may feel to be a frustratingly early end to the design process. Some designers of large and complex systems involving long time scales are now beginning to view design as a continuous and continuing, rather than a once and for all process. Perhaps one day we may get truly community-based architects for example who live in an area constantly servicing the built environment as doctors tend their patients.

2 *There is no infallibly correct process*

Much though some early writers on design methodology may have wished it, there is no infallibly good way of designing. In design the solution is not just the logical outcome of the problem, and there is therefore no sequence of operations which will guarantee a result. The situation, however, is not quite as hopeless as this statement may suggest. We saw in chapter 6 how it is possible to analyse the structure of design problems and in the next section we shall explore the way designers can and do modify their process in response to this variable problem structure. In fact we shall see how controlling and varying the design process is one of the most important skills a designer must develop.

3 *The process involves finding as well as solving problems*

It is clear from our analysis of the nature of design problems that the designer must inevitably expend considerable energy in identifying the problems confronting him. It is central to modern thinking about design that problems and solutions are seen as emerging together rather than one following logically upon the other. The process is thus less linear than implied by many of the maps discussed in chapter 3 but rather more argumentative. That is, both problem and solution become clearer as the process goes on. We have also seen in chapter 6 how the designer himself is actually expected to contribute problems as well as solutions. Since neither finding problems nor producing solutions can be seen as predominantly logical activities we must expect the design process to demand the highest levels of creative thinking. We shall discuss creativity as a phenomenon and how it may be promoted in the next section.

4 *Design inevitably involves subjective value judgement*

Questions about which are the most important problems, and which solutions most successfully resolve those problems are often value-laden. Answers to such questions, which designers must give, are therefore frequently subjective. As we saw in the discussion of the Third London Airport in chapter 5, how important it is to preserve churches or birdlife or to avoid noise annoyance depends rather on your point of view. However hard the proponents of quantification, in this case in the form of cost benefit analysis, may argue they will never convince ordinary people that such issues can rightly be decided entirely objectively. Complete objectivity demands dispassionate detachment. Designers being human beings find it hard to remain either dispassionate or detached about their work. Indeed designers are often aggressively defensive and possessive about their solutions. Perhaps it was this issue above all else that gave rise to the first generation of design methods; designers were seen to be heavily involved in issues about which they were making subjective value judgements. However this concern cannot be resolved simply by denying the subjective nature of much judgement in design. Perhaps current thinking tends more towards making the designer's decisions and value judgements more explicit and allowing others to participate in the process, but this path too is fraught with many difficulties.

5 Design is a prescriptive activity
One of the popular models for the design process to be found in the literature on design methodology is that of scientific method. Problems of science however do not fit the description of design problems outlined above, and consequently the processes of science and design cannot usefully be considered as analogous. The most important, obvious, and fundamental difference is that design is essentially prescriptive whereas science is predominantly descriptive. Designers do not aim to deal with questions of what is, how and why, but rather with what might be, could be and should be. While scientists may help us to understand the present and predict the future, designers may be seen to prescribe and to create the future, and thus their process deserves not just ethical but also moral scrutiny.

6 Designers work in the context of a need for action
Design is not an end in itself. The whole point of the design process is that it will result in some action to change the environment in some way, whether that be by the formulation of policies or the construction of buildings. Decisions cannot be avoided or even delayed without the likelihood of unfortunate consequences. Unlike the artist, the designer is not free to concentrate exclusively on those issues which seem most interesting. Clearly one of the central skills in design is the ability rapidly to become fascinated by problems previously unheard of. We shall discuss this difficult skill in the next section.

Not only must the designer face up to all the problems which emerge he must also do so in a limited time. Unlike the scientist, the designer is often not free to decide that he needs more information, rather he must get on and make the best of a bad job. Design is often a matter of compromise decisions made on the basis of inadequate information. Unfortunately for the designer such decisions often appear in concrete form for all to see and few critics are likely to excuse mistakes or failures on the grounds of insufficient information. Designers, unlike scientists, do not seem to have the right to be wrong. While we accept that a disproved theory may have helped science to advance we rarely acknowledge the similar contribution made by mistaken designs.

PART THREE

DESIGN THINKING

8 Types and Styles of thinking

The highest possible stage in moral culture is when we recognise that we ought to control our thoughts.

Charles Darwin, *The Descent of Man*

The art of reasoning consists in getting hold of the subject at the right end, of seizing on the few general ideas that illuminate the whole, and of persistently organizing all subsidiary facts around them. Nobody can be a good reasoner unless by constant practice he has realised the importance of getting hold of the big ideas and hanging onto them like grim death.

A. N. Whitehead, *1914 Presidential address to the London Branch of the Mathematical Association*

Theories of thinking

In this section we shall turn our attention from the study of design problems to those who solve them: designers. What kinds of people make good designers, and what kinds of attitudes, skills and abilities do they bring to bear on the problem? Of all the questions we can ask about design the matter of what goes on inside the designer's head is by far the most difficult and yet the most interesting and vital. This leads inevitably into the realm of cognitive psychology, the study of problem solving and creativity, in short of thought itself. Thinking is one of the most notoriously intractable parts of psychology since the thought process is not easily observed. It need not be started by, nor concerned with current events in the environment, and moreover it need not conclude with any communication to the outside world. The designer, however, has never resembled Rodin's "Thinker" who sits in solitary meditation, but has in contrast always externalised his thoughts, not only as an end-product in the form of a design, but as an integral part of the process itself in the form of drawings and sketches. The whole purpose of doodles, sketches or models is to act as a kind of additional memory to freeze and store spatial ideas which can then be evaluated and manipulated. These drawings and models, taken together with interviews with designers and their writings, offer some insight into the thought processes involved in design. In successive chapters we shall look in detail at the designer's thought processes in terms of his philosophy, general strategy and specific techniques. However first we shall briefly review the way psychologists have studied and classified the thought processes which we may expect to comprise the act of designing.

No subject can have attracted more contrasting theories throughout the history of psychology than the phenomenon of human thought. The great behaviourist Thorndike believed that human intelligence comprises only one basic process, the formation of associations. Since his early writings many behaviourist psychologists have tried to explain thinking purely in terms of direct associative links between stimuli and responses. Watson even went so far as to argue that thinking is really only subvocal speech or "talking to ourselves". Indeed Jacobsen and Marx found evidence of peripheral muscular activity during thinking, but of course, failed to show that this was actually the thinking itself. Hull modified the idea, suggesting that the muscular activity was so small as to have no effect save to act as feedback to the thinker. The idea behind such an apparently curious notion was that in this associationist model of thought each of our responses could be fed back to act as another stimulus eliciting yet a further response. Writers such as Osgood (1952) and Berlyne (1965) eventually abandoned the search for "muscular thought" and introduced the notion of purely cortical responses. For Berlyne, patterns of thought result from us choosing from a variety of responses which we associate with each stimulus. The choice is made simply by selecting the strongest associative link although these links can be strengthened or weakened by our experience of life.

In essence the behaviourist view is that it is unnecessary to hypothesise a complex mental mechanism where behaviour can be explained without one. The question of course is: can the behaviourists adequately explain intelligent thought? In fact their theories have appeared most successful in explaining behaviour such as learning and the acquisition of physical skills. The rat in the psychologist's maze can be seen as learning to associate the response "left" or "right" with the stimulus of each junction. Thorndike expanded this simple idea by placing cats in puzzle boxes where a variety of bolts or catches needed to be released to open the cage. The cats escaped by trial and error and thus apparently learned to solve a problem. Behaviourists have thus tended to explain problem-solving or goal directed thinking in terms of successive mental trial and error. Actually the associationist model of thought seems more applicable to imaginative thought or daydreaming. Here the thinker is not wilfully controlling direction but is rather allowing his thoughts to wander.

However satisfactory or not their theories may be the behaviourists have contributed little which may be used by the designer wishing to improve his thinking skills. By contrast, the Gestalt school of psychology established a tradition of studying problem-solving which is continued today by such writers as Edward De Bono. Gestalt theories of thinking concentrate on processes and organisation rather than mechanisms. Wertheimer (1945) saw problem-solving as grasping the structural relationships of a situation and re-organising them until a way to the solution is perceived. This already begins to sound more like designing than Thorndike's cats, but Wertheimer went even further. He maintained that this mental re-organisation of the situation is achieved by applying various modes of attack such as redescribing the problem and the use of analogous situations. As we shall see later this forms the essence of a number of quite recently proposed design techniques. Whereas the behaviourists used animals to explain thought the Gestaltists used animals to show the absence of human-like thought. The Gestaltists were also very interested in perception and therefore stressed the importance of context in thought. De Groot's (1965) use of words in describing Kohler's experiments with apes is most revealing.

We humans are struck by the inability of these otherwise quite intelligent animals to take a ring off a nail; a possibility that we immediately *see*. Due to our experience with nails and rings and their usage, we *see* the situation in a totally different way than the ape does. Similar examples can be given touching upon the relation between adults and children.

Thus for De Groot thinking depends upon acquiring the ability to recognise relationships, patterns and complete situations. In his study of chess De Groot shows how experienced chess players "read" situations rather than "reason them out" as do the less experienced. The chess master can play so many games simultaneously simply because each time he sees a board he is able to recognise the pattern of the game. This "schooled and highly specific way of perceiving" combined with a "system of reproductively available methods in memory" produces a rapid and inscrutable response which, to the unitiated observer, looks like an intuitive flash of genius. Paradoxically, the chess master may also spend far longer examining a situation than his less experienced counterpart simply because he can see more problems, perhaps further ahead, than the average player.

Markus (1969) listed four basic sources of information available in a design decision-making situation: the designer's own experience, others' experience, existing research and new research. It is perhaps the inevitable mixing of these sources which contributes to designers' seemingly random behaviour, sometimes apparently intuitively leaping to conclusions whilst at other times making very slow progress.

The Gestalt psychologists paid particular attention to the way we represent the external world inside our heads. Most notably Bartlett in his now classical studies of thinking (1958) and remembering (1932) developed the notion of an internalised mental image which he called the "schema". The schema represents an active organisation of past experiences which is used to structure and interpret future events. In a series of experiments in which Bartlett asked subjects to remember drawings and reproduce them perhaps several weeks later, he showed how such memory is dependent on the drawings being meaningful. That is, we must have already formed the appropriate schemata in advance to interpret and appreciate events. More recently, developmental psychologists such as Bruner and Piaget have shown how human thought processes develop in parallel with the child's formation of such basic and fundamental schemata.

The advent of electronic communication devices and information processing machines such as computers has generated a new perspective on human thought. Information theory has provided a metric which allows the amount of information processed during a problem to be measured. Psychologists have attempted to uncover the mechanisms with which we think by measuring our performance on simple tasks against the amount of information processed. Such writers as Posner appear to bridge the gap between the behaviourists and Gestaltists by concentrating on mechanisms while still viewing thinking as a strategic skill. Garner's influential book on cognitive psychology reports experiments in short term memory, discrimination, pattern perception, and language and concept formation all using information theory to provide the yardstick for human performance. Other workers in this field have proposed theories of human problem solving based on the model of the computer program. The most famous application of this technique being the G.P.S. (General Problem Solver) program of Newell, Simon and Shaw (1958). Such programs cause the computer to exhibit behaviour resembling such hitherto peculiarly human characteristics as "purpose" and "insight". This at least shatters some of the mystique surrounding work on thought processes by showing how sequences of very elementary information transformations could account for the successful solution of complex problems. Whether such simple processes are actually the basis of human thought is of course still open to considerable doubt. Unfortunately there are limitations to the usefulness of such computer programs as models since they rapidly become as complex as the processes they model.

The new cognitive approach to human thinking sees man as a much more adaptable and genuinely intelligent organism than the early behaviourist approach. It deals with process and operational function rather than physical mechanism, and it stresses the influence of the context in which problems are perceived on the thought process itself. The cognitive psychologists, while building on the Gestalt tradition, also follow on from the first flush of enthusiasm shown by psychologists for applying information theory to human thought, but are rather less fanatical about its potential. In his brilliant treatise on cognitive psychology Neisser (1967) points out that humans are different from machines from the very beginning of the perceiving and thinking process: "humans ... are by no means neutral or passive towards incoming information. Instead they select some parts for attention at the expense of others, recording and reformulating them in complex ways." As we shall see in later chapters this phenomenon of our selective perception of problems has exercised the minds of many design methodologists who seek to devise ways of broadening designers' perceptions.

Perhaps the most important feature of the cognitive psychology approach to thinking is the new recognition of the existence of some kind of executive controlling function in the mind. Since cognitive psychology accepts that information is actively reorganised and reconstructed in memory rather than passively recorded and recalled, it follows that something must control this process. The existence of such an executive function was denied not only by classical association theory but also by the Gestaltists, however more recent work on artificial intelligence has shown how executive routines in computer programs can control the order in which a very complex sequence of operations are performed in extremely flexible and responsive ways. There is not space here to do justice to this profound and fascinating subject but the interested reader will find brilliant and readable discussions of the matter in *Plans and the Structure of Behaviour* (Miller, Galanter and Pribram 1960) and the *Ghost in the Machine* (Koestler 1967). If the cognitive psychologists prove to be right about such an executive then we may expect to discover much more about the way we design since it is clearly the executive which is responsible for switching our attention from one part of a problem to another or allowing us to reorganise our perceptions in new ways. As we shall see these are vital skills for the designer.

The cognitive theorists' approach to thinking is also attractive to those who seek to understand the design process because it draws many parallels between thought and perception. Both primary and secondary processes are postulated, the primary thought process being a multiple activity like parallel processing in computers. These crudely formed thoughts are similar to the preattentive processes in vision or hearing, being only drawn to our conscious attention if selected for detailed and deliberate elaboration by the secondary processes. It is in the secondary processes where all the real work is done. These processes have to be learnt and developed and are obviously dependent upon what is already memorized and the way material has been organised in primary processing. The cognitive theories thus lay great emphasis upon the way we organise perceived information and store it. Failure to recall is seen as analogous to a failure to notice something in a visual scene. Thus attention in perception and thought is seen as responsible for directing our thoughts and thus crucial to problem solving. This theme will be taken up again in a rather less theoretical and more practical way when we consider methods of stimulating creativity and improving problem solving skills in design.

Types of thinking

In his classic treatise on the human mind Ryle (1949) observes that "thinking" is a polymorphous concept. Like the term "farming", Ryle suggests, "thinking" embraces many different kinds of activity which may have little in common. Just as one farmer may be milking his cows while another reaps his crops, so two thinkers may not necessarily appear to share common activities. Psychologists have tended to study thinking by attempting to divide and classify types of activity which could be investigated separately. Perhaps the most well used division is that between "reasoning" and "imagining", both of which are obviously needed in design.

When "reasoning" the individual is said to carry out mental operation within some coherent symbolic system. Reasoning is considered purposive and directed towards a particular conclusion. This category is usually held to include logic, problem-solving and concept formation. When "imagining", on the other hand, the individual is said to draw from his own experience, combining material in a relatively unstructured and perhaps aimless way. Artistic and creative thought as well as daydreaming are normally considered imaginative.

This kind of simplistic taxonomy is perhaps as misleading as it is apparently helpful. If reasoning and imagining were truly independent categories of thought one should not be able to speak sensibly of "creative problem-solving" or a "logical artistic development", which are both quite meaningful concepts. Many kinds of problems, even in such apparently logical disciplines as engineering, can be solved creatively and imaginatively. Certainly art can be logical and have well developed structure. Indeed it is even possible to study the structure of art forms using the logic of information theory (Mueller 1967). Only rarely can one find an instance in the real world outside the psychologist's laboratory when one kind of thought is employed in isolation. The mode of thinking employed is obviously very much dependent on the nature of the situation. Most writers have concentrated on two main related factors, the thinker's relation to the external world, and the nature of the control he exercises over his thought processes.

Murphy (1947) suggested that mental processes are bipolar, being influenced both by the external world and by inner personal needs. In his study of personality Murphy was particularly interested in the individual's susceptibility to these two influences, and the resultant predominance of certain thinking styles which could be observed in the individual. The normal person is rarely entirely preoccupied by either one of these influences for any amount of time but rather alternates between the two. It is, however, possible to identify conditions under which one would expect the normal person to attend more to one influence than the other.

Problem-solving obviously requires more attention to the demands of the external world than to inner mental needs. In imaginative thinking on the other hand the individual is primarily concerned with satisfying his inner needs through cognitive activity which may be quite unrelated to the real-world. This seems to offer the psychological distinction between design and art as discussed earlier. Design is directed towards solving a real world problem while art is largely self-motivated and centres on the expression of inner thoughts. This does not mean that imaginative thought can be excluded from the design process but that its product will probably always need evaluation by rational thought in order that the designer's work should be relevant to his real-world problem. The control and combination of rational and imaginative thought is one of the designer's most important skills and we shall discuss this crucial issue further in the next chapter on creativity.

A very popular approach to the study of human intelligence is represented by the factorial school. This work holds that human intelligence is not a simple factor but rather a whole series of related factors each of which may be present to greater or lesser extents in any individual. In his review of such work Guilford (1956) concluded that intellectual factors could be divided into the two major groups of thinking and memory. The thinking factors, which are of most interest here, Guilford further subdivided into cognition, production and evaluation.

The cognition factors of human thought have to do with becoming aware of and understanding classes of objects or ideas. This analytic ability to classify and recognise is of the utmost importance in everyday thought. For example it would not be possible to study the differences between the structural systems employed in romanesque and gothic churches unless one could first recognise and classify such buildings. Guilford maintains that there are three ways of developing such a class system depending on whether the figural, structural, or conceptual content is used. Thus one might recognise a class by its figural properties. Children may initially recognise all four-legged animals as cows and only later look for further detail such as horns or tails. The second system of class recognition, by structural content, requires some functional relationship to exist between class members such as in the "complete the series of symbols" type of I.Q. test question. Finally one might recognise a class conceptually, such as architects or lawyers as being a group of people having passed certain examinations. For Guilford then, these cognition factors influence our ability to define and understand problems whether they be to do with the appearance, function or meaning of objects. As Guilford himself points out, problems of figural and structural types abound in design and the ability to discriminate figural and structural classes is likely to be important to the designer.

Guilford's second group of thinking factors is concerned with the production of some end result. "Having understood a problem we must take further steps to solve it" (Guilford 1967). Just as Guilford's cognition factors deal with the ability to recognise figural, structural and conceptual order so the production factors hypothesise our ability to generate or produce these three kinds of order, but Guilford found that the reality was not quite as neat as the model suggested: "In the investigation of planning abilities it was hypothesised that there would be an ability to see or to appreciate order or the lack of it, as a feature of preparation for planning. It was also hypothesised that there would be an ability to produce order among objects, ideas or events, in the production of a plan. A single ordering factor was found."

Thus Guilford found not two abilities to handle structure or order, but one which seemed to belong amongst the production factors rather than the cognition factors. This is a most interesting observation in the light of Lawson's (1972) experiments quoted earlier which tended to show that architects discover about the structure of their problems by attempting to generate order in their solutions, and lends more weight to the argument that analysis and synthesis in design should not be regarded as entirely separate activities. Unfortunately few psychologists seem to have considered both the recognition and production of order at the same time so for the time being we must accept the distinction since the literature on productive thinking has several useful concepts to offer the student of design.

Productive thinking and design

When Wertheimer (1959) introduced the notion of "productive thinking" he was primarily concerned with the directional quality of thought; "what happens when, now and then, thinking forges ahead?" He showed with a whole series of small experiments how, when in a problem situation, thinking can be productive if it follows an appropriate direction. There are at least two fundamental questions which the experimental psychologist can ask here. Is the thinker trying to control the direction of his thinking and if so is the direction productive or not?

It is clear that mental processes are bipolar in their directional quality just as in their relation to the external world. The thinker can wilfully control the direction of his thought or he can allow it to wander aimlessly. The normal person does not solely engage in either one kind of thought, but rather varies the degree of directional control he exercises. Here is another distinction between design and art. The designer must consciously direct his thought processes towards a particular specified end, although he may deliberately use undirected thought at times. The artist however, is quite able to follow the natural direction of his mind or to control and change the direction of his thinking as he sees fit. Bartlett's (1958) classification could be used to support this argument distinguishing as it does between the artist's thinking and that of the designer: "There is thinking which uncovers laws of finished structure or of relations among facts of observation and experiment. There is thinking which follows conventions of society or of the single person, and there is other thinking still which sees and expresses standards."

Clearly the search for, and expression of, standards forms an important part of artistic thought. The designer must primarily indulge in Bartlett's first kind of thinking in order that he can appreciate the relationships between the given elements of his problem. The amount of purely expressionistic thinking he may do is largely a function of the degree to which he is allowed to generate his own constraints. As we have seen this varies considerably from problem to problem and there will thus inevitably be many instances when design and art are indistinguishable with this test.

Bartlett goes on to suggest two main modes of productive thinking which he calls "thinking in closed systems" and "adventurous thinking". A closed system, in Bartlett's definition, has a limited number of units which may be arranged in a variety of orders or relations. Formal logic is such a closed system as are arithmetic, algebra and geometry. Closed system thinking can be highly creative as in the case of discovering new mathematical proofs or making anagrams. Bartlett identifies two processes in closed system thinking, interpolation and extrapolation. Here again we see the concept of the directionality of the thought process:

Genuine thinking is always a process possessing direction. In interpolation the terminal point and at least some evidence about the way there are given, and all that has to be found is the rest of the way. In extrapolation what provided is some evidence of the way; the rest of the way and the terminal point have to be discovered or constructed. So it is in extrapolation that directional characters or properties are likely to become most prominent.

Although these two processes of interpolation and extrapolation are attractive concepts, when we consider real world design conditions the situation loses some of its clarity. Rarely in design does one know or not know the terminal point but rather one has some information about it; it is a matter of degree. In some kinds of design one knows exactly where one will end up, in others one has very little idea.

Bartlett's other mode of productive thought, adventurous thinking, is less clearly defined than thinking in closed systems. In this mode of thought the repertoire of elements which can be considered is not prescribed. Indeed, adventurous thinking often depends for its success upon elements not normally related being brought together in a new way, hence its adventurous nature. Yet again however the distinction between adventurous thinking and thinking in closed systems becomes blurred when applied to design situations. It is certainly possible to find examples of closed system problems in design if we look for them. The problem of arranging tables and chairs in a restaurant certainly requires thinking in closed systems. Often, however, such examples do not bear too close an examination for rarely does the designer work exclusively with a kit of parts. If a particular arrangement of tables will not fit, the designer may often be free to try different sizes or shapes of tables or even alter the shape of the restaurant! Thus the ensemble of elements in design problems is usually neither entirely closed nor entirely open. In fact we often recognise a creative response to a design problem as one where the designer has broken free of a conventionally restricted set of elements. Thus the rigid imposition of closed systems as in the case of system building is seen by many designers as a threat to their creative role.

Throughout much of the literature on productive thought we find a variety of closely related binary divisions between on the one hand rational and logical processes and on the other hand intuitive and imaginative processes. These two major categories have become known as convergent and divergent production. Typically the convergent task requires deductive and interpolative skills to arrive at one identifiably correct answer. Convergent ability is measured by many of the conventional I.Q. test problems and has been associated with ability in science. The divergent task demands an open ended approach seeking alternatives where there is no clearly correct answer. Divergent ability can be measured by tests mistakenly called creativity tests such as "how many uses can you think of for a brick" and divergent ability has been associated with skill in the arts. As we shall see in the next chapter these two ideas have frequently been grossly oversimplified and variously confused with intelligence and creativity. Guilford (1967) and others treat convergent and divergent thinking as separate and independent dimensions of ability which can occur in any proportions in an individual. Guilford maintains that, although few real-world tasks require exclusively convergent or divergent thought, the distinction is still valid and useful.

From our analysis of the nature of design problems it is obvious that, taken as a whole, design is a divergent task. Since design is rarely an optimisation procedure leading to one correct answer clearly divergent thinking will be required. However there are likely to be many steps in any design process which themselves pose convergent tasks. True, such steps may eventually be retraced or even rejected altogether, but it would be absurd in the extreme to pretend that there are no parts of design problems which are themselves amenable to logical processes and having more or less optimal solutions. Design clearly involves both convergent and divergent productive thinking which is probably what makes it so challenging and satisfying to practise.

9 Creative thinking

It is a well known fact that all inventors get their first ideas on the back of an envelope. I take slight exception to this, I use the front so that I can include the stamp and then the design is already half done.

Roland Emett

A very great deal has been said and written about the phenomenon of creativity and yet it stubbornly remains one of the most unclear, perhaps even confused, concepts in the literature of the psychology of thinking. Some stress the importance of disecting the act of creation by attempting to chart a map similar to those of the design process already discussed. Other writers concentrate on the apparently enormous individual differences in the level of creative talent which we possess, with some even trying to identify the "creative personality". Other writers see creativity as a skill which must be developed and practised. Associated with this group are those who present techniques or systems of promoting creative thought. This variety of ideas leaves us with many problems of definition. What do we call creative? Is it the individual, whether it be a Beethoven, a Picasso or an Einstein, and if so are such great talents born or do they develop? Can we rightly call the end product of their efforts creative whether it be a symphony, a painting or a theory? Do such people employ an identifiably different mode of thinking which itself we should describe as creative?

It is generally accepted that design is a creative occupation and that good designers are themselves creative people, and certainly we often describe their work as creative. In our study of creativity in design then we need to examine not only products but also processes and persons.

Our assessment of the creativity of a product is notoriously subjective. There is no reliable scale of the creativity of things or ideas. Even worse, we tend to assess the creativity of an idea in terms of our personal reactions to the idea itself. As De Bono (1976) puts it:

"creativity is a value word and represents a value judgement – no one ever calls creative something new which he dislikes." It is through products that we most easily recognise creativity and yet the product itself rarely tells us much about how it came to be. While a new scientific theory or an original piece of design are both valuable and useful in themselves neither are particularly helpful to the would be theoretician or designer in telling him what he should do. There are other problems with studying products. Rarely is one mind responsible for the entirety of a creative product. There is much discussion these days of the plight of the lone inventor who is unable to get the support he needs to develop an idea. But where does the creativity lie in the innovative process? Should we only describe the inventor as creative or should we include all those who refine, develop and realise that idea? Such questions begin to direct our attention away from the product to the person. Are some people naturally good at getting novel ideas while others are better at the development and elaboration of ideas? Do these two talents go together or do they involve quite separate mental processes?

The earliest attempts to describe the creative process were made not by psychologists but by thinkers such as Helmholtz and Poincaré. These early descriptions emphasise several changes in thinking style thus dividing the process into phases. Poincaré (1924) tells of a period of initial investigation of the problem followed by a period of apparent rest. The solution, he claims, then appears in a sudden and unexpected manner needing further conscious elaboration, development and verification. As a result of such anecdotal descriptions many psychologists have attempted to classify the stages of creative thinking. Although the terminology varies most writers seem to agree on a five stage process consisting of: "first insight", "preparation", "incubation", "illumination" and "verification".

The period of "first insight" (Kneller 1965) simply involves the recognition that a problem exists and a commitment is made to solving it. This period may itself last for many hours, days or even years. The formulation of the problem may often be a critical phase in design situations. As we have seen, design problems are rarely initially entirely clear and much effort has to be expended in understanding them thoroughly.

The next phase of "preparation" involves much conscious effort to develop an idea for solving the problem. (MacKinnon 1976) As with our maps of the design process it is recognised that there may be much coming and going between these first two phases as the problem is

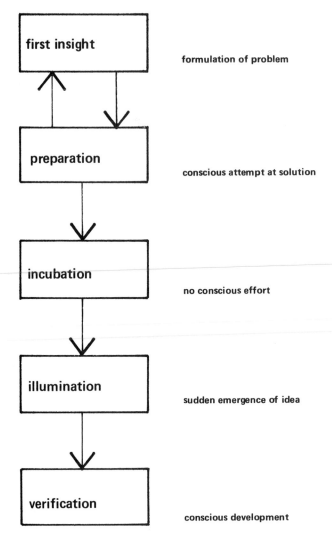

first insight	formulation of problem
preparation	conscious attempt at solution
incubation	no conscious effort
illumination	sudden emergence of idea
verification	conscious development

9.1   The five stage model of the creative process

reformulated or even completely redefined. Yet all these writers emphasise here that this period of preparation involves deliberate hard work and is then frequently followed by a period of "incubation" which involves no apparent effort, but which is often terminated by the sudden emergence of an idea ("illumination"). Some authors (MacKinnon 1976) explain this as unconscious cerebration during the incubation period. The thinker is unwittingly reorganising and re-examining all his previous deliberate thoughts. Other writers suggest that by withdrawing from the problem the thinker is then able to return with fresh attitudes and approaches which may prove more productive than continuing his initial thought development. Once the idea has emerged all writers agree upon a final period of conscious verification in which the outline idea is tested and developed.

Although many of the authors of these models of the creative process have emphasised that they do not see the various phases as temporally discrete there is still a strong sequential and linear element in such models. The strong emphasis on the inspirational moment is perhaps as much based on our romantic archetypes of creative acts as it is on reality. Whilst the Eureka syndrome is by no means uncommon it is not the only way to develop what we recognise as a creative idea. The famous and acclaimed engineer Barnes Wallis is obviously no Pythagoras for he tells us: "There has always been a problem first. I have never had a novel idea in my life. My achievements have been solutions to problems ... things have never come in a flash: they come only as a result of months, even years, of very heavy work." (Whitfield 1975).

Studies of gifted individuals generally recognised as creative fail to provide evidence of any obvious and clear process at work. However other studies which concentrate on individuals themselves rather than the process do reveal interestingly consistent results. Roe (1952) concluded that exceptionally creative scientists are characteristically very intelligent and persistent, and highly motivated. They are also confident, self-sufficient and assertive. Designers have been popular targets for such studies for, as MacKinnon (1962) puts it:

It is in architects, of all our samples, that we can expect to find what is most generally characteristic of creative persons ... in architecture, creative products are both an expression of the architect, and thus a very personal product, and at the same time an impersonal meeting of the demands of an external problem.

MacKinnon found his creative architects to be poised and confident though not especially sociable. They were also characteristically intelligent, self-centred, outspoken and even aggressive. They also hold a very high opinion of themselves and MacKinnon (1976) concludes that if he could only ask one question of an individual to determine how creative he was that question would be "are you or are you not creative?" Rather disturbingly, perhaps, it was MacKinnon's sample of architects judged to be less creative who saw themselves as more responsible and with a greater sympathetic concern for others! In terms of abilities many such studies show creative designers and artists to be unusually perceptive and observant with an ability to concentrate hard but also easily shift attention from one thing to another. As we shall see later, many of the design techniques used to promote creative thought are based on the simple idea of shifting the designer's attention and changing the context within which he perceives the problem.

Experience and creativity

One of the most vexed and perennial questions in design education concerns the balance between the free, open-ended and expressive work demanded of the student, and attention to the acquisition of knowledge, discipline and experience. Many experimental psychologists have provided evidence which shows that the effects of experience on problem-solving are not always beneficial. The early Gestalt psychologists Wertheimer, Duncker and, in particular, Maier (1931) showed the almost universal tendency of experience to have a mechanising effect on individual thinking. That is, each problem is not viewed afresh but rather is first classified according to types of problem already encountered, and the solution selected accordingly. Only if the problem type cannot be recognised is there any serious attempt to study it in any depth. Luchins and Luchins (1950), who see such mechanization as the establishment of a habitual mental set or "Einstellung" report a series of attempts to reduce such effects by concretizing abstract problems. In one set of tasks numbers representing volume were replaced by a range of jars of various capacities and subjects performed simple arithmetic by pouring milk from one jar to another to obtain a specified quantity. Luchins and Luchins found that subjects rapidly came to use certain combinations of jars in consistent ways and thus adopted a mechanical approach and consequently they often performed more pouring operations and wasted more milk than was necessary for a particular computation. From these and many other similar studies the evidence is clear that experience of problems perceived as similar all too readily leads to a mechanization of thought whereby we try to fit old solutions to new problems. This is the very antithesis of creativity, and has always been a matter of great concern for designers. Since few design problems are completely novel how can a designer avoid the mechanizing effect of being so familiar with so many previous solutions?

In industry the need to improve perhaps already successful products provides the ultimate test of creative thinking. The mechanical, channelized thinking described here is the very opposite of what is required. It is this stimulus which has provided two of the most famous of all "creativity techniques"; Brainstorming (Osborn 1957) and

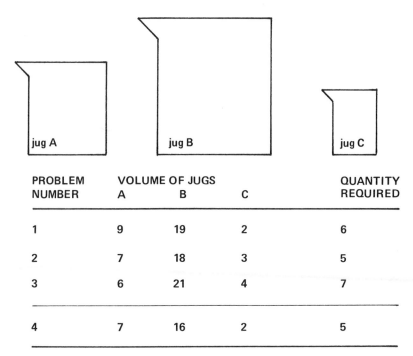

| PROBLEM | VOLUME OF JUGS | | | QUANTITY |
NUMBER	A	B	C	REQUIRED
1	9	19	2	6
2	7	18	3	5
3	6	21	4	7
4	7	16	2	5

9.2   The problem is to achieve the quantity required by using only the three jugs. After a series of problems like 1,2,3 in which the answer is B-A-2C subjects were too mentally mechanised to spot that a solution to the problem can more easily be achieved by A-C

Synectics (Gordon 1961). Both these techniques are based on the simple idea of using a group of minds acting in concert so as to avoid any individual mechanisation of thought. In both cases there are very tight rules of permitted behaviour and participants are reprimanded by the group chairman for adopting judgemental attitudes but are encouraged to build on the ideas of others. Participants are also encouraged to generate as many different ideas as possible no matter how absurd or wild they may seem. Research has shown (Meadow and Parnes 1959) that Brainstorming can generate more ideas which are judged to be better, but the technique has also been criticised for leading to superficial results through a lack of a provision for analysis of the problem. Synectics is a much more elaborate technique than Brainstorming having some nine major phases. The early stages of Synectics concentrate on the investigation and reformulation of the problem, leaving solution generation until the later stages. In fact Synectics is too complex a technique to describe here, and participants require considerable training. Perhaps for this reason Synectics has not become widely popular outside limited commercial circles where regular use can be made of established teams of trained participants. However the central theme of the technique, the deliberate use of analogy, is one we shall return to later. Four types of analogy are employed in synectics: personal, direct, symbolic and fantasy analogy.

When using personal analogy the problem solver identifies personally with some part of the problem or solution, thus acting out the situation. For example in the design of a chair this approach might lead the designer actually to feel where the loads and stresses are imposed and thus to gain a new perspective on the structural design of the chair. The direct analogy allows for the use of parallel facts or systems to help understand the problem. This can be particularly useful where the problem is abstract and can be concretized and visualised as with a water flow model of electricity. In symbolic analogies the designer identifies not himself but some other object with some part of the situation. Thus to return to the example of the chair it could be viewed as a giant toadstool or a bale of straw and in either case the designer may be able to shake himself free from the mechanizing effect of so many four-legged chairs. Fantasy analogy allows the designer to suspend his sense of credulity and to explore temporarily the seemingly fantastic or impossible.

This last idea of fantasy is central to many creativity techniques. It depends on the temporary suspension of the critical judgements we all make based on past experience. Many ideas from the zip fastener to space flight must have seemed fantastic prior to their realisation. Unfortunately it is often the case that the more expertise and experience we have the more fantastic such ideas appear since we can more readily see the difficulties. Design students, with their naivity and lack of experience, can thus often be more creative than their more practised elders. As a lecturer in electronic engineering once put it to me when describing the many genuine inventions made by his students in their project work: "They make such breakthroughs because they don't yet know that it can't be done!"

Intelligence and creativity

Underlying some of the literature on creativity is the notion that creativity is itself a single talent or gift held in varying quantities by different people. Even a brief and superficial examination reveals this to be a grossly oversimplified idea. Very few people are able to perform creatively in more than one or two fields of endeavour. Creativity is not just skill or talent but is also related to context; the situation within

draw the next square in the series

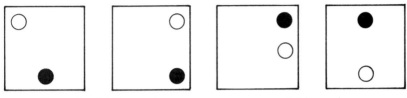

9.3 Conventional I.Q. tests have one correct answer and this requires convergent reasoning

what could this drawing represent?

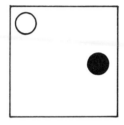

9.4 The so called "creativity tests" have many acceptable answers and thus require divergent reasoning

which the person perceives the problem and performs the process. As we have seen, experience and familiarity are likely to be important factors in determining the creativity of our response to a given problem. Similarly motivation and the sense of urgency or the cost of failure can work to inhibit or release creative potential. What then is the role of intelligence in creative performance? Is creativity always associated with intelligence, are the two attributes independent or perhaps even in conflict? Obviously a certain minimal level of intelligence is essential for any creative work for without basic intelligence problems cannot be identified and understood. Mackinnon (1962) in his studies of creative people records that "no feeble-minded subjects have shown up in any of our creative groups." Whilst this may seem quite obvious from our own personal experience we may not so readily recognise MacKinnon's other conclusion that being more intelligent does not guarantee an increase in creativeness.

The first important contribution to this argument comes from Getzels and Jackson (1962) who contrasted the characteristics of children who scored highly on conventional intelligence tests and those who did well on so called creativity tests. Getzels and Jackson claimed to have identified many differences between the two groups not least of which was the image of the children held by both themselves and their teachers. The "highly intelligent" children were conforming and compliant and sought the approval of their elders, while the "highly creative" children were more independent setting their own standards and values and were less well liked by their teachers. There have been many technical criticisms of Getzels and Jackson's work with doubts raised about their methodology but what is of most interest to us here is their use of the terms "intelligence" and "creativity".

The tests employed by Getzels and Jackson could be more accurately described as tests of convergent and divergent thinking. As we saw in the last chapter the conventional I.Q. test is composed of questions to which there is one correct answer whereas the so-called creativity tests require many answers to each question. Getzels and Jackson's children then were good either at convergent or divergent thinking rather than necessarily being highly creative or intelligent.

Hudson (1966) has shown that schoolboys with high convergent abilities tend to be drawn towards the sciences while their more divergent counterparts are more interested in the arts. Thus, unless we are to abandon the notion of a creative scientist we must reject Getzels and Jackson's implicit conclusion that creativity is exclusively a function of divergent thinking ability. In fact Hudson (1968) has argued that each problem situation generates its own requirements for convergent or divergent thinking; "each field has its own waveband of emotional openness; only within this range of openness which each waveband affords are certain degrees of openness or restriction more conducive to good work than others." Only in the psychologist's laboratory do we find tasks requiring either convergent or divergent thinking to the exclusion of the other.

Although generally associated with divergent thought, art is by no means solely dependent upon the generation of new ideas. As Hedge and Lawson (1979) have pointed out some artists work in an entirely original and creative way while, others may follow traditions, developing ideas but not breaking fundamentally new ground. Not all artists are generally considered highly creative, but even those that are clearly demonstrate qualities of perseverance and single-mindedness not usually associated with divergent thought. Turner must surely rank as one of England's most creative painters. His work records scenes and events prolifically and simultaneously portrays light and colour in an entirely original and unique way. It is essential creativity that causes us to single out Turner for our admiration above the many in English painting, and yet we cannot accuse Turner of a flight of ideas or even of being prolific in ideas. His lifetime's work shows a dedicated, perhaps

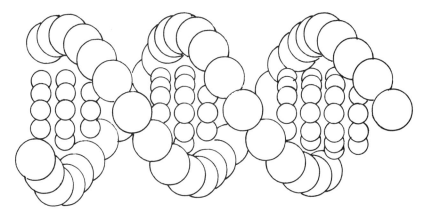

9.5   The double helix of DNA was not discovered by purely convergent reasoning

even obsessional, concentration on developing the technique of suggesting transmitted light on the solid canvas.

Just as it is too simplistic to view art exclusively as the exercise of divergent thought so science cannot be explained entirely as convergent thought. One of the most creative scientists of all time, Einstein, arrived at his revolutionary theory of relativity by connecting the two previously well developed but quite unrelated concepts of mass and energy. James Watson in "The Double Helix" (1968) presents a most fascinating account of the creative scientist at work. Watson and his colleague Francis Crick discovered the extraordinarily complex and beautiful structure of DNA. The mental processes revealed by Watson certainly do not fit with the archetypal image of the convergent reasoning of scientists. In fact the structure of DNA could not simply be deduced from previously gathered evidence and at least one great leap into the unknown was required. That essential and precious element of divergent thought was the key which would unlock a whole sequence of convergent trains of thought. This is by no means so uncommon a phenomenon in science as we often believe. Just as Einstein's and Watson's ideas were not the evolutionary result of a deductive process but rather the revolutionary outcome of a divergent leap so are many major advances in science. Kuhn (1962) has analysed the development of science as a series of revolutions which take place as the result of a conflict between the forces of established tradition and innovation. Kuhn argues that science clings to established paradigms while they creak at the joints until eventually the conventional wisdom collapses in the face of a wholly new paradigm not growing obviously and gradually out of the old but rather by sudden and dramatic revolution.

Creativity and design

Creativity then, can be seen not simply as the ability for divergent thought but rather a balance of convergent and divergent thinking abilities appropriate to the situation. The truly creative scientist needs something of the artist's divergent thought to see new possibilities while for his part the artist needs to be able to apply the single-minded perserverence of the scientist to develop his ideas. What makes design such a challenging task psychologically is the very even balance of these two sets of mental skills that are needed to produce creative work. As a rough guide it seems likely that the more important the designer-generated constraints are then the more the designer will need to employ divergent thinking skills. Just as design problems vary so do the skills and abilities of designers. Some prefer the free open-ended kind of problem where there are few imposed constraints and the imagination can be let loose, while others are more at home with more tightly constrained problems. It is important for the designer to recognise the nature of the problem and to employ reason and imagination, convergent or divergent thought in appropriate doses.

The appropriate dose however is not always easily decided, but practice usually gives experienced designers a good feel for the situation. The beginner, however, may have to analyse more self-consciously the nature of the problem: the model developed in chapter 6 is intended to assist this process. Although creativity should not be associated exclusively with divergent thinking creative work always depends on at least one vital spark of imagination. It is perhaps better therefore for the designer to use divergent thinking in excess rather than too sparingly. For most people it is easier to think convergently than divergently on demand. Reason is more easily controlled than imagination and the results of free imaginative thought can readily be subjected to rational evaluation later. Techniques for stimulating imaginative divergent thought will be dealt with in more detail in a later chapter.

Some of the discussion here about experience and creativity raises difficult questions concerning the development of creativity in design education. Since experience can so easily have the effects of mechanizing thought and limiting ideas, should design students be exposed to existing solutions and the work of other designers? For example is it right that architectural students working on a housing project should first study established house types and site layout arrangements? There are bound to be conflicting points of view on this issue. Certainly some will argue that concentrating on previous solutions

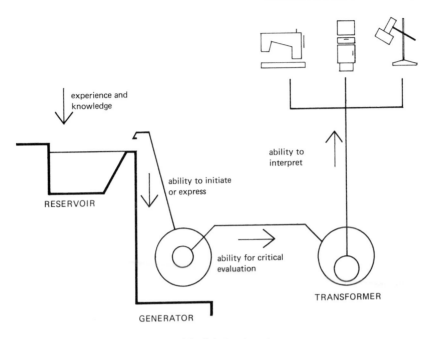

9.6   Laxton's hydro-electric model of design learning

will seriously inhibit the students' ideas. Others will point out the obvious mistakes that students will make in the absence of such studies, but this argument is sometimes countered by the contention that one's own mistakes provide more lasting and meaningful lessons than studying model answers. Perhaps in the end a lot depends upon our view of the role of student project work. Do we set students design problems in order for them to learn about design or to demonstrate their ability in design. Necessarily this issue is just as clouded, for in most design courses the project work provides not only the central part of the education but also represents the major element of assessment.

Laxton (1969) in a discussion of design education in schools suggests that children cannot expect to be creative without a reservoir of experience. He uses the analogy of a hydro-electric plant to explain his three stage model of the skills taught in design courses. Laxton's first skill, the ability to initiate or express he claims is dependent on having a reservoir from which to draw ideas. Laxton argues that it is only later that the student has the power to evaluate and discriminate between these ideas. Interpretation is the third and final skill in Laxton's model and is analogous to the transformer stage of his hydro-electric plant, allowing ideas to be translated into appropriate forms and contexts. Thus for Laxton creativity in design is promoted by initially concentrating on filling the reservoir with a supply of ideas. This is very much in step with psychologists writing on creativity. Kneller (1965) goes so far as to say: "One of the paradoxes of creativity is that, in order to think originally, we must familiarise ourselves with the ideas of others. ... These ideas can then form a springboard from which the creator's ideas can be launched."

10 Design philosophies

Form follows function.

Louis Sullivan

To some the functional was equated with the utilitarian, to some with the expressive, to others it was identified with the geometric, to still others with the organic or the efficacious.

A B Handler, *Systems Approach to Architecture*

When studying design methods and techniques it is sometimes easy to forget that the mind of the designer continues to function outside the design studio. Of course we should really view designing as one of the many mental activities performed by designers rather than in the splendid isolation suggested by books such as this! The significance of this rather simple observation lies in the influence of wider thoughts and attitudes on the design process itself. Although they are often ill-formed and not easily articulated we all of us tend to have attitudes towards issues which are wider than any one design problem and therefore influence our approach to these more specific problems. In particular, designers usually design not just because they enjoy doing it but also because they tend to be fascinated by the sort of things they create. This fascination cannot help but lead to a study which itself generates a collection of attitudes, which we will here call philosophies, which in turn must be seen to have their effect on the design process itself. In particular the view that a designer takes of his role in society and the function and reason for his work are crucial to any real understanding of the process he employs. To illustrate and explain this argument we shall turn to a series of fascinating articles in which leading architects of their time describe their approach to architecture. In these articles, which were published at the rate of about three a year from 1965 in the RIBA Journal, we are able to see something of the great variety of philosophies that can coexist even within the mainstream of architectural thought. In this context we are most interested not in the philosophies themselves but in what these general views suggest about the nature of the design process.

Running throughout much of this material there can be found a debate on the nature of the user's needs and his role in the design process. Denys Lasdun (1965) tells us that "our job is to give the client ... not what he wants but what he never even dreamt he wanted" while Bob Maguire (1971) feels that "the primary object of the creative architectural process is to achieve – to use Lethaby's phrase – 'nearness to need'." These two generally expressed attitudes can be seen to give rise to discernably different ways of working. As Lasdun himself says "what I have previously said about the client affects the methodology of design." Lasdun describes this methodology as a series of models made at each stage which can be shown to the client for discussion. The models may indicate space and form but not appearance, although Lasdun recognises that "each member of the (client) committee will be dressing that skeletal model up as he thinks it is going to look." On the other hand Maguire tells us that "one thing which is essential ... is to get the brief formulated in terms of needs rather than solution images ... while you postulate the solution-image, you are preventing an exploration of needs in depth." Thus while Lasdun exchanges ideas with his client in the language of solutions, particularly in model form, Maguire prefers to discuss the client's needs more through the language of problems, and these differences of method arise out of a general attitude towards the role of user needs. Either of these approaches could be contrasted strongly with attitudes which lie outside the mainstream of architectural thought. For example Mitchell's (1972) belief that "the models used by design and planning specialists are quite difficult for laymen to understand, and this forms a considerable barrier to their effective participation in the design process" leads him to experiment with computer techniques which allow users access to much more powerful models of the environment which they can actually manipulate themselves. Others like Rod Hackney (1976) take an even more participatory view of the design process and see the designer in the role of supporting the users in the implementation of their wishes. The design process resulting from this attitude takes the architect out of his isolated studio to live in the community which he sees himself as serving.

Thus we can see that the way information is exchanged during a design project is to a large extent a function of the client and designer's views of their respective roles. This hardly suggests a universally applicable design method and thus, far from agreeing with Gregory (1966, quoted earlier) that there is "a process the pattern of which is the same whether it deals with the design of a new oil refinery, the construction of a cathedral, or the writing of Dante's *Divine Comedy*," we may conclude that many quite different processes may be used even in the design of a simple house.

Attitudes towards user's and the designer's role can also give rise to quite different views of the start or finish of the design process. James Stirling (1965) is quite explicit about a feeling that many designers must have shared, that of possessiveness for a finished product which has been so important throughout the creative process but now belongs to others "when the clients are about to move in I have a sort of resistance. I think they are going to do all the wrong things when they get inside. I keep coming back and hanging around and probably pester the daylights out of them." For example Stirling tells us how "disillusioned" he was when the occupiers of his flats at Ham Common plastered the brick fireplaces thus destroying Stirling's consistent use of brickwork inside and out. By contrast with Stirling, Herman Hertzberger (1971) believes that buildings should be consciously designed to facilitate this process of people "taking possession". "What we should make is the wall on which everyone can write whatever he wants to communicate to the others." For Hertzberger the design process does not end with the conclusion of the designer's work: "However far the designer goes, the occupants will go on making the building after they have taken it over, changing it again and again and steadily taking more and more possession of it." This leads Hertzberger away from an optimising view of the design process, where each element is designed to perform its specified function, towards a process where functions are combined deliberately, perhaps even wilfully, into more open-ended and flexible forms. For example Hertzberger shows how in a housing scheme a concrete block can serve to house a light fitting, act as a stand for milk bottles or even as a table or chairs for an outside meal. Hertzberger is quite prepared to accept that the form is not ideal for any one purpose but is rather a compromise.

This seems a long way from the "form follows function" dictum of the modern movement and raises another important aspect of these general philosophies; our attitudes towards certainty and doubt in design. Some designers have held very strong beliefs about the rightness of what they are doing. All manner of strongly argued sets of principles have been used to justify and defend styles of design. Watkin (1977) in his most readable account of *Morality and Architecture* has revealed

the absurdity of some of these trenchantly held views. As Watkin puts it, many of these arguments "point to the precedent of Pugin when they suggest that the cultural style they are defending is an inescapable necessity which we ignore at our peril and that to support it is a stern ethical and social duty." Certainly Pugin's famous defence of the

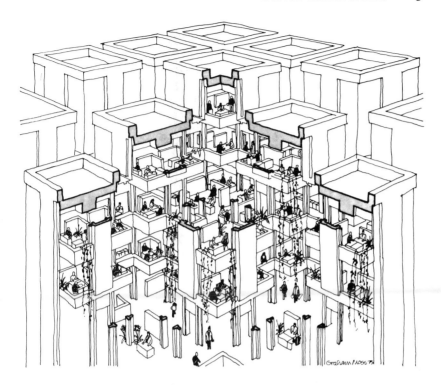

10.1(a),(b) Hertzberger's flexible multiple functions: offices of Centraal Beheer, Appledorn, Holland, designed to encourage the occupants of the building to "take possession" of it (above and opposite)

Victorian Gothic revival is argued not solely in terms of its structure or functional advantages but also in a chauvinistic and even pseudo-religious vein; "if we view pointed architecture in its true light as Christian art, as the faith itself is perfect, so are the principles on which it is founded." (Pugin 1841). Victorian gothic is no longer seen as unequivocally having "right on its side" and such statements may now seem transparently absurd, but it is easy to forget that similar sentiments have been expressed much more recently. The modern movement in architecture with its emphasis on simplicity based on lack of ornament, together with its international influence, is perhaps not recognisable as a style in the tradition of architectural development, but it has been adopted and defended with all the crusading fervour of Pugin and his followers. Gropius (1935) concluded his essay on *The New Architecture and the Bauhaus* with the sublimely confident assertion that "the ethical necessity of the New Architecture can no longer be called in doubt," and James Stirling (1965) tells us that as a student he

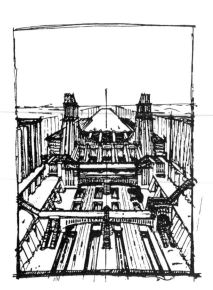

10.2   Sant Elia's drawings showed a futuristic Utopia created by the use of advanced technology

"was left with a deep conviction of the moral rightness of the New Architecture".

In contrast to all this certainty and assertion Paul Koralek feels that his practice of Ahrends, Burton and Koralek are like many others in that they "work in a general atmosphere of uncertainty". (Burton, Ahrends and Koralek 1971). "We can no longer function in the context of the certainty and conviction of the modern movement, and are surrounded by doubts and questions", he tells us, and Maguire (1971) seems to agree when he speaks of "the doubts we must all feel about architecture's performance in the recent past". These fundamentally opposed viewpoints are reflected in the designers' approach to actual problems. Describing his buildings Stirling is quite clear that the circulation organises the building form in each case whereas Koralek admits to making decisions "largely without knowing how". We shall return to this central issue of what method the designer

uses to organise and structure his thinking in the next chapter but for
the time being we can see that the existence or not of organising
principles whether they be of the gothic style or the modern movement
is highly influential in determining design method.

In their more philosophical writings designers often reveal the
importance of their attitude towards the future as an influence on the
design process. As Cedric Price (1976) puts it: "in designing for
building every architect is involved in foretelling what is going to
happen". The designer's view of the future is often very much bound
up with his attitude towards progress and, in particular, the use of
technology. Some idolize technology while others remain suspicious of
change. In the second decade of this century the futurist movement in
art spilled over into design through the work of the Italian architect
Sant-Elia. His love affair with the dynamics of modern life centred
around an obsession with transportation, movement and speed. In his
1914 *Manifesto of Futurist Architecture* Sant-Elia declared that "we
must invent and rebuild ex novo our modern city like an immense and
tumultuous shipyard, active mobile and everywhere dynamic, and the
modern building like a gigantic machine". There are no doubts here
about the benefits of advanced technology and the individual is clearly
seen as subservient to the inevitable onward march of progress. Not
surprisingly these attitudes were soon to take the Futurists down the
road to Italian Fascism although very little of their vision was ever
realised. More recently, and slightly less fanatically Weinberg (1966)
has restated the often implicit link between enthusiasm for technological
progress and right wing political ideology. "Technology has provided a
fix – greatly expanded production of goods – which enables our
capitalist society to achieve many of the aims of the Marxist social
engineer without going through the social revolution Marx viewed as
inevitable." Weinberg goes on to argue that technology has thus
"fixed" the problems of poverty and, through the invention of the
nuclear deterrent, has also "fixed" the problems of war. As Cross
(1975) comments "Weinberg is apparently suggesting that a belief in
technology is demonstrably a superior or more effective belief than
either Marxism or Christianity". But the opponents of advanced
technology can be just as dramatic in their claims. Dickson (1974) in
his championing of "alternative technology" lists page after page of
accusations levelled at our technological society. "The individual in
contemporary society feels himself increasingly trapped by powerful
forces outside his control. He is reduced to little more than an economic
cipher, continuously and uncomprehendingly manipulated within a

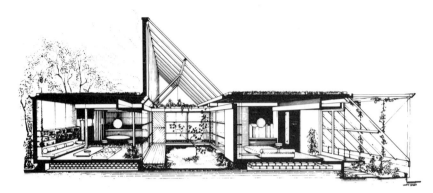

10.3 This drawing by Cedric Green of the Sheffield University Experimental Solar heated house shows a more questioning but still idealistic view of future possibilities

vast, inhuman complex. Technology, originally developed as a means of raising man above a life of poverty, drudgery and ill health, now shows its other face as a threat to his sanity and survival.'' The anti-technologists have their utopian dream which is every bit as visionary as Sant-Elia's Citta Nuova, but for them the new life is based on renewable energy sources, organic agriculture, cottage industry and small-scale community government.

The argument between high and alternative technology is not itself important here but rather what is of interest is the effect of such strongly held beliefs on the design process. Much as we would like to, it is not possible for us to question all our assumptions every time we design. What unites the "advanced" and "alternative" technology advocates is their shared assumption that a particular kind of technology is desirable in itself. In one case this may lead to the conscious exploitation of new materials and factory-based manufacturing techniques whereas the opposite view demands the use of low energy materials and labour-intensive methods. Either approach considerably narrows down the range of design solutions at the outset and generates an image of the solution every bit as restrictive as the influence of style already discussed. Indeed sometimes the individual design problem seems subservient to the continuing needs to develop the technology. Norman Foster (1970), famous for his uncompromisingly machine-like architecture, tells us that "ideally we would like to see ourselves as bridging the gap between the potential of new ideas, both technological and operational, and their practical realisation". Foster describes one of his designs as "a vehicle for further exploring a systems approach to multi-use buildings". Thus we can see that, although designers may be commissioned and briefed by clients and may chiefly concern themselves with the needs of users, the design process is also performed for the satisfaction of the designer himself. Rand (1970) identifies this duality in his discussion of graphic design: "Because advertising art, in the end, deals with the spectator, and because it is the function of advertising to influence him, it follows that the designer's problem is two-fold: to anticipate the spectator's actions and to meet his own aesthetic needs."

In this respect all design can be at least partly regarded as an exercise in propaganda, for it is through his work that a designer can most easily explore and simultaneously disseminate his ideas. Indeed for many it is the only viable channel of communication. "It is difficult for us to speak of our work, because we have maintained that most of what we have to say is in our buildings" (Burton, Ahrends and Koralek, 1971). Eric Lyons (1968) is clearly worried by the influence of too strong a set of beliefs on design. He thinks that "there is far too much moralizing by architects about their work and that too often we justify our ineptitudes by moral postures". For Lyons "buildings should not exist to demonstrate principles". Judging by their writings few of his contemporaries would agree.

Perhaps we should conclude this brief chapter with the reminder that the whole design methods movement itself represents a set of attitudes which have deliberately been used to influence the designer's process. Jones (1970) seems in no doubt that new design methods are needed when he tells us that "the writings of design theorists imply that the traditional method of design-by-drawing is too simple for the growing complexity of the man-made world". In the early nineteen sixties many writers seemed convinced that the methods of science were applicable to design and that design could and should be treated as an observably logical process: "it seems not unreasonable to hope that the whole discipline of system engineering may serve as a paradigm for a rational theory of design" wrote Gosling in 1963. Ten years later Broadbent (1973) was to devote the whole of his chapter on "new attitudes to design" to a history of the philosophy of science and to justify this with the assertion that "the reasons for approaching design in new ways ... are determined by shifts in philosophical attitudes which are not exclusive to architecture, but pervade the whole of our culture and, most specifically its science and technology". Underlying much of this

10.4 Does an "orderly method of working" or systematic design necessarily imply system building techniques? The Nottinghamshire County Office building

"first generation" literature on design methods then, run two basic attitudes. First, that designers are, by and large, not equipped with adequate methods. One is frequently left with the view that designers and in particular architects, are a pretty incompetent lot who stagger from one problem to the next not really knowing what they are doing. The second assumption of the first generation methodologists was that designers could be helped by the introduction of more self-conscious systematic procedures. The overtly logical disciplines of science and systems engineering were frequently paraded as having honest, reliable and respectable methodologies which could and should be applied to design. A reflection of these views in practice can often be seen in the writings of the architects who immersed themselves in the large scale public sector practices which gave rise to industrialised building systems which were to be mass produced and could be built on any site for almost any purpose. Dan Lacey, one of the leading figures in this movement described his basic philosophy towards the design process in one of the RIBA "architect's approach to architecture" lectures.

Feelings of fire in our bellies have to be controlled by an orderly method of working. Our administrative colleagues and expert clients are sometimes fascinated by our ability to develop new ideas, but, on the other hand, they will not really be confident about us if they feel that we are people who work in a muddle and arrive at our ideas in a haphazard way. We must recognise that our clients are people who have probably evolved an orderly approach to their own field of work. We must display the fact that although we are emotionally interested in the problems of design we are also as concerned as they are about factual issues such as cost planning, contractual arrangements and site operations. (Lacey 1965).

More recently this approach has been criticised for confusing method with end product. Systematic design, it has been argued, does not necessarily imply system building, although some would go so far as to suggest that industrialised system building is only acceptable if the designer is prepared to deny his "emotional interest" in design! Whatever view one takes in this argument it is certainly not clear that the new design methods or their reflection in systems of construction have really solved any major difficulties. On the whole, designers are probably just about as good or bad as they were twenty years ago, but there can be no doubt that the design methods movement has left its mark. Bob Maguire (1971) feels that "there is a certain pressure to pretend that designing something is a kind of scientific process". In fact Maguire argues that all this philosophising far from helping designers, actually seems to add further perplexities and insecurity to the situation.

For the architect, the complexity of his milieu is compounded by a confusion of values in which means are mistaken for ends and given inflated importance: methodology in the design process, for example, or industrialisation, modular co-ordination, or even metrication. None of these disciplines is to be dismissed, but the tendency to dogmatically pronounce one or more of them to be the road to salvation can be seen as a retreat to a position of apparent certainty in the face of the insecurity of the context in which we work.

By now it should be apparent to the reader that the author of this book takes the view that as much can be learnt about the design process from studying what experienced designers say and do as from the writings of design methodologists. It is not the intention exclusively to endorse any of the views expressed in this chapter but rather to show that design methods should not be considered without some understanding of the general philosophy of the designer himself.

11 Design strategies

The act of making an architectural decision can perhaps be stripped of its mystique, while some far more viable set of operations is seen to add up to something – not a style, not even a discipline, but some indefinable aggregate of operations which have been intelligent and appropriate and have given a situation its fourth dimension.

Peter Cook, *Architecture Action and Plan*

In the last chapter we examined the recent philosophical writings of some well known architects which reveal a great variety of ideas about architecture. Many more such views could have been presented, including the ideas of those rather less committed to conventional architectural practice. The intention was simply to suggest that it is not necessary to include revolutionary or fringe ideas about architecture in order to find considerable variation in approach to the design process. This hopefully acts as a counterbalance to the earlier section of the book when emphasis was laid on the more theoretical writings of design methodologists. If we are to gain any real insight into the complexities of the design process both practitioners and methodologists have much to tell us, and yet apparently they often seem in conflict.

Essentially the message from the methodologist seems to be one of generality and standardisation. In chapter three, for example, we examined some maps of the design process which purport to show a route from the beginning to the end which it is assumed will be taken by all designers. The message from the practitioners is rather different. They speak less of the RIBA plan of work and rather more of their own individual interests, approaches and strategies. Our earlier examination of some maps of the design process suggested that whilst many seemed quite logical none were really all that useful. The writings of practitioners confirm the view that there is not one route through the design process but many. However it is not enough to rely entirely on designers' accounts of what they do. If we could accurately describe what goes on in our head when we design then there would be no need for any books on design methodology! The methodologists have given us concepts and a language with which to analyse and study design strategies but we must always remember that it is the practitioners who actually design.

In this chapter we will examine some of the ways in which designers actually approach specific design problems rather than their more generalised views and attitudes discussed in the last chapter. We are not concerned here with the detailed mechanisms for dealing with various parts of the design process but rather the overall methodology or strategy. Just as designers' generalised philosophies are varied then so are their more particular strategies. It is important here to remind ourselves of the major variables which comprise the design situation. At the beginning of the book we saw how design is frequently classified in terms of solutions or end-products and how designers are usually restricted to one group of solution types by the limitations of their technological expertise. Thus architects know how to design buildings, engineers bridges and so on. Although it seems nonsense to classify design in terms of the solution which only exists after the design process, it would be idle to ignore the importance of preconceptions about the solution. Both clients and designers usually have at least outline notions about the solution from the outset. As we saw from the last chapter designers often have ongoing interests which they bring to bear on individual design problems even to the extent that particular designs can be seen merely as "vehicles" for developing these ideas.

Not only the problem but also the solution and the designer himself all influence the design situation and the strategy employed. In fact one of the major ways in which strategies can be seen to vary is the way the designer focuses his attention on either the problem or the solution. We saw earlier how many of the more theoretical design process maps suggest that analysis of the problem precedes synthesis of the solution. We also saw how empirical evidence suggests that designers actually tend to use more solution-focused approaches. In the light of our examination of the nature of design problems and solutions in chapter 7 this seems to be more logical that perhaps it at first appears. The critical features of design here are that problems can seldom be comprehensively formulated and that solutions cannot be logically derived from them. Most design problems are simply too complex for the designer to hold all the factors and variables in his mind at once, so the real difficulties are: where to begin and then how to proceed. In other words what sort of strategy to employ.

Most design strategies seem to begin with a brief scanning of the problem as it appears initially. Agabani (in preparation) studied the strategies used by architectural students by video-recording group design sessions. He found that it was rarely very long before such phrases as "this suggests ..." or "we could try ..." and so on were in common use. Each aspect of the problem was thus checked to see if it suggested ideas for the solution. Eastman (1970) in his "analysis of intuitive design processes" presents the protocols of designers working on a new bathroom. His subjects invariably started drawing solutions almost immediately.

An examination of protocols obtained from such closely observed design sessions reveal that most designers adopt strategies which are heuristic in nature. The essence of this approach is that it is simultaneously educational and solution seeking. Heuristic strategies do not so much rely upon theoretical first principles as on experience and rules of thumb. The architectural students in Lawson's (1979) experiments with coloured blocks described in chapter 3 used heuristic or trial and error procedures. The science students used classical information-search strategies calculated to reveal as much information as possible about the rules relating the blocks. The architects on the other hand first built the most attractive solution and tried it out. If this initial attempt did not work the architects compromised, modifying it until an acceptable combination of blocks was obtained. To illustrate this principle further let us look at two methods of sizing timber floor joists. In the first, theoretical, method calculations are performed using the known compressive and bending stress capabilities and elasticity of the timber. The calculations give a depth of timber which will not deflect more than 0.003 of the span and will not cause the bending and sheer stresses to exceed the permitted levels. The calculations are based on established theories of structural mechanics and would be performed by structural engineers and required for building regulation approval. The alternative to this precise but laborious procedure is to use our second, rule of thumb method. There are many possible rules such as "the depth of 50 mm wide joists at 400 mm centres is 25 mm for every half metre of span". Such a method is by no means precise but will never be very far out. However not only does the method go straight to the solution but it is educational in the sense of clearly identifying the critical relationship between depth and span of the joist. The rule of thumb is also much more practical in that timber is not available in an infinite range of depths but only in 25 mm increments.

This rule of thumb provides a good model of the heuristic strategy so

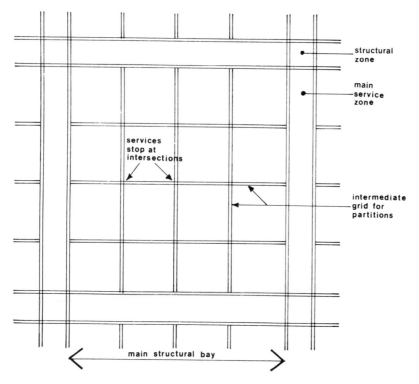

structural
zone

main
service
zone

services
stop at
intersections

intermediate
grid for
partitions

main structural bay

11.1   The first approach to the office building

commonly employed in the environmental design fields. A rough idea is quickly developed for the most significant elements of the solution which can then be checked by more precise methods and adjusted as necessary. The model breaks down in that, whereas it is fairly obvious that the depth and span of a joist are the most critical elements, it is by no means so easy to decide what is critical in a building, an interior or urban development. Indeed what is important or critical is likely to be a matter of opinion. To see how this might actually work in practice we shall briefly consider the approach taken by three groups of architecture students towards a competition to design a large new county authority office building.

After a fairly short period of work the groups presented their ideas and thoughts so far. The first group started by describing how they felt that the environmental requirements of the office space were the critical factors. They had done a literature review of all the research they could find on office space and had arrived at a sketch design of a "typical bay" showing the structural and service systems for providing shelter,

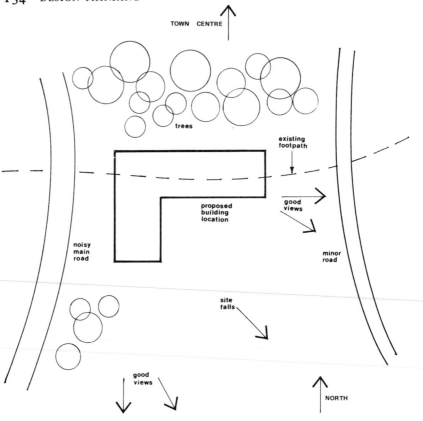

TOWN CENTRE

trees

existing
footpath

proposed
building
location

good
views

noisy
main
road

minor
road

site
falls

good
views

NORTH

11.2   The second approach to the office building

power, comfort and light while maintaining a relatively interrupted floor space to give flexibility of layout. The building they thought could be assembled by replicating these bays as desired and as the site permitted.

By contrast the second group took the view that office space itself was not difficult to design and they had focused their attention on some rather unusual features of the site. The suburban parkland site was located between two major radial roads connected by a footpath. This group had noticed that the competition brief had stressed the importance of not presenting a remote or forbidding image to the ratepayers. They decided to build their office around a covered mall which followed the line of the footpath and thus brought the public right through the building. Taken together with the banks of trees, south facing slope and considerations of screening noise from the busy roads this enabled our second group to develop proposals for the siting and massing of their building. The next phase, they explained, would be to fit the various departments into the building adjusting the envelope where necessary.

The third group had also focused on the visitors rather than just the regular inhabitants of the building. This group were anxious to avoid what they saw as the usual failings of such buildings, that is presenting large inscrutable facades with unclearly structured interiors which are easy to get lost in. For them the whole structure of the organisation provided the stimulus to building form. Each section and department were to be clearly articulated using a hierarchy of open spaces linked by well defined routes to a central entrance court.

It is rather difficult to decide whether any of these approaches are better than the others and it is certainly not possible to declare any to be either right or wrong. Although at first sight these three approaches may seem rather different, in fact they share basically the same overall strategy. In each case a group of sub elements of the overall problem have been clustered together and elevated to the role of form generator.

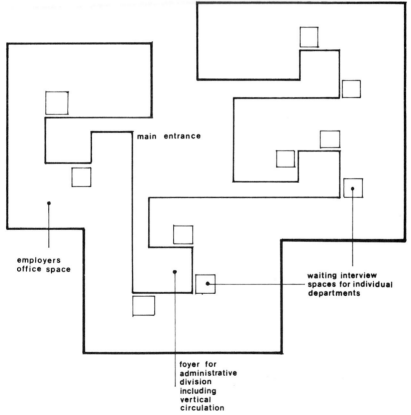

main entrance

employers
office space

waiting interview
spaces for individual
departments

foyer for
administrative
division
including
vertical
circulation

11.3   The third approach to the office building

What differentiates the three is simply the kind of constraint which has been used in this focal role. The first and last group concentrated on the way the building should be organised by focusing on internal constraints while the second group looked at the external constraints imposed by the site. The first and second groups looked at constraints generated by two different types of user, the employee and the ratepayer. The first group gave priority to the efficient control of the working conditions and thus recognised mainly radical constraints. By contrast the second group thought that the quality of the place was more important and they recognised more symbolic constraints. The third group when questioned saw no conflict between these and felt that the physical expression of the organisation achieved in their building would not only be easy for the ratepayer to relate to but would also lend a sense of identity and belonging to the employees thus creating a good social working environment.

These three examples of design strategies come from a collective or group process, and it is worth noting that the use of individuals and groups in design is itself a matter for strategic planning. The value of group working will be discussed in more detail in chapter 13. Attitudes towards the role of groups in design are often polarised. Barnes Wallis (Whitfield, 1975) is quite sure that "good design is entirely a matter of one single brain", while the engineer John Baker (Whitfield, 1975) who developed the design and build organisation IDC, tells us that "working in this completely integrated team is as thrilling as any experience I have ever had". Moulton, the designer of the famous bicycle, values group working in commercial product design but only after a technical concept has been originated by an individual. On the other hand Robert Opron (1976), the designer of Citroen and Renault cars, believes in team work from the outset: "The real problem is to find executives who are prepared to accept discipline and to subordinate themselves to the interests of the final product."

After all this study of the design process one is often left with a feeling that somehow the major issue has been avoided. Few practising designers with whom I have discussed the design process seem to have found much value in many of the early design methods. Perhaps this is understandable in the same way that a professional musician is not likely to find value in a basic instrumental tutor; he has already learnt to do all that can be communicated in such a remote and formal fashion. However there is more to the designers' suspicion of such methodology than that. What frequently disappoints designers seems to be the methodologists' failure to deal with the central problematic issue of the generation of three-dimensional form. There are many published techniques for identifying, analysing and restructuring problems and for comparing and evaluating solutions, but, with the exception of the open-ending thinking methods such as Brainstorming, Synectics and Lateral Thinking, there is little help with the actual creation of physical form from a set of abstract relationships. Even such tools as the so-called "creativity techniques" such as Brainstorming cannot themselves directly assist with form generation but really only provide a mental atmosphere conducive to the free flow of ideas. How then is this translation actually achieved in practice?

We have seen how the range of possibilities can be restricted by initially focusing attention on a limited selection of constraints. In the examples considered so far those constraints have been mainly radical in function. That is to say they are considerations of the primary purpose of the object being designed. The architectural student groups designing a county administrative office building focused their attention on providing satisfactory working conditions and internal communications. Another popular focus of attention is provided by the more solution-oriented practical constraints. These constraints are imposed by the properties and performance of the materials, structures and systems used in the physical solution. The extent to which practical constraints dominate the process is likely to be a function of the type and complexity of the technology involved. Mario Bellini (1977), the designer of the Olivetti golfball portable typewriter, emphasises the difference between designing static artifacts such as furniture, and mechanical or electrical goods in this respect. Obviously the product designer must learn to adapt his process according to the situation. As design generators these constraints are helpful to the designer seeking to create physical form for two reasons. Firstly the practical constraints are themselves not abstract but largely concrete and three-dimensional and therefore actually suggest form. Since the practical constraints are concerned with making the solution they suggest not only overall forms but other features such as methods of jointing and fixing. Even secondary issues such as access for maintenance can be used by the designer to generate form. The Pompidou Centre in Paris with its explicitly colour-coded pipes and ducts expressed as major elements both within the building and on the facades is an obvious example.

The second attraction for the designer of concentrating on practical contraints is their constancy. The principles of structure or weathering do not vary from problem to problem and are thus amenable to long term study and the development of standard responses. We saw in

11.4(a),(b) The Pompidou Centre in Paris seems to have been generated by a concentration on the expression of practical constraints

chapter two how the vernacular process gave rise to design developed in this way. The igloo and the cartwheel were both formed around the materials and technology available at the time. More recently, advanced

11.5 The first cast-iron bridge of Abraham Darby at Coalbrookdale in 1779 is very reminiscent of the stone arch

technology and new synthetic materials have had a liberatory and inspirational effect on designers, although it often takes some time for the practical constraints associated with a new material to be fully understood. Thus when Abraham Darby built his first cast-iron bridge at Coalbrookdale in 1779 his design imitated the pattern of the then more familiar stone arch rather than exploiting the properties of the new material. Indeed the histories of architecture and engineering are largely governed by man's increasing mastery of applied mathematics, his developing understanding of materials and his ever more sophisticated constructional technology. A study of temples and cathedrals throughout the ages will reveal as much about the practical constructional constraints as about the radical liturgical constraints of the time.

More recently architects have often become particularly interested in the use of particular materials such as steel, timber, concrete or glass and have developed systems of construction and building form from the constraints imposed by the properties of these materials. Le Corbusier (1946) for example declared that "reinforced concrete has brought about a revolution in the aesthetics of construction. By suppressing the roof and replacing it by terraces, reinforced concrete is leading us to a

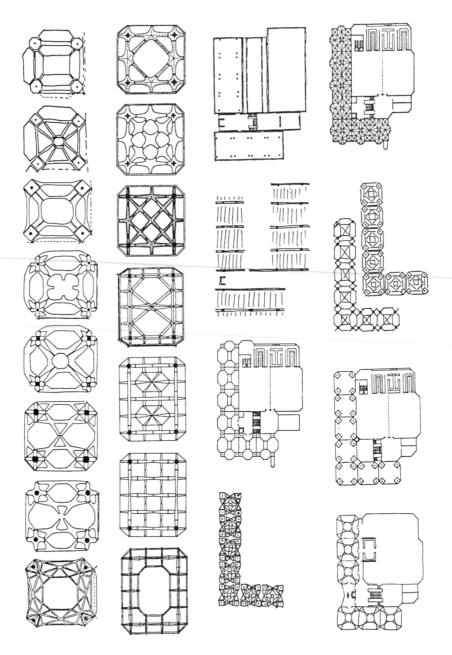

11.6   Bill Howell called his approach to design "vertebrate architecture", and relied chiefly upon structure to generate form as shown by these studies for the University Centre building at Cambridge

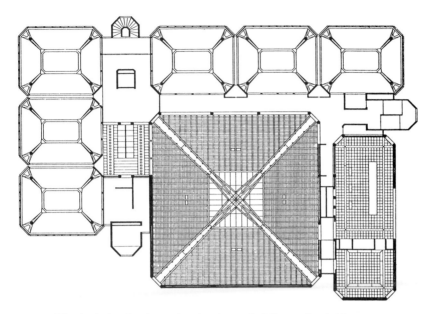

11.7 The final plan for the University Centre building at Cambridge

new aesthetic of the plan, hitherto unknown." Le Corbusier thought it necessary to develop "a new basis of construction established in logic": only then he argued would a new architectural aesthetic be able to grow.

Practical constraints used as form generators can be derived not just from specific materials but also from more generalised attitudes towards structural and constructional methods. Bill Howell (1970) described how his practice of Howell, Killick, Partridge and Amis have adopted a philosophy of building what they describe as "vertebrate architecture" in which "the interior volume is defined and articulated by actual, visible structure". Howell showed how this led to a design process in which architect and engineer worked in close dialogue to develop the anatomy of each building. At first glance this approach seems rather wilful and indeed Howell admits that "we do it, because we like it". This seems to suggest a design process organised around designer generated practical constraints, and certainly clients and users do not get mentioned too often in Howell's article. But the matter is obviously not so clearly compartmented in Howell's mind because he tells us that:

While thinking about structural economy, the relationship of internal partitioning to downstanding beams, the relationship of cladding to the structure, and so on, you are taking decisions which affect the relationship of the anatomy of the building to its site and to its neighbours.

Thus we are left with the impression that an approach to structure is simply the tool that this particular designer has chosen to open up each design problem; it generates form which can be tested against other less physical constraints.

This brings us from the practical to the formal constraints. In Howell's work the boundary is blurred since the structure which holds up his floors and roofs is also used to create the formal articulation of spaces internally and masses externally. However it is quite possible to take a far less practical view of formal constraints as design generators. In their study of "the geometry of environment" March and Steadman (1974) explore many applications of mathematics to describe spatial organisation in design. The book shows how geometry may be used to understand both abstract and concrete formal relationships. Such branches of mathematics as topology and boolean algebra can handle relationships which can exist independently of three dimensional space whilst the more conventional geometries can be used to study such physical transformations as reflections or rotations. With such techniques designers can explore how shapes and solids may be combined by stacking, nesting and fitting to create complex structures and spaces. For March and Steadman such a study seems to become an end in itself but they suggest that their work could lead to new mathematical methodologies in design practice. Critchlow (1969) in his book *Order in Space* makes virtually no attempt at all to explain how his catalogue of shapes and solids might actually be used by a designer. He simply describes his undoubtedly fascinating journey through geometry as "one way to approach order in space". The sub-title "a design source book" suggests that formal geometry, like constructional principles, can be studied independently of design problems in order to accumulate a reservoir of ideas which can be drawn on when actually designing. March and Steadman (1974) show how formal constraints derived from geometrical principles can have both intellectual and practical significance in design. For example the use of deliberately limited sets of dimensions can create the possibility of both proportional systems and modular co-ordination. Undoubtedly the human intellect is stimulated by the witty use of proportion whether it be in music or design, and modern mathematics in the form of information theory has given us many new tools for understanding our perceptions of complex patterns and sequences. However the psychology of the perception, as opposed to the creation, of design is another subject beyond the scope of this book. By contrast the advantage of modular-co-ordination in which disparate elements can reliably be related to each other in a variety of ways with economy and simplicity of jointing are more practical and much simpler to appreciate.

One of the most famous proportioning systems proposed for use by designers is Le Corbusier's Modulor. In essence this is simply a Fibonacci series; a mathematical progression, certainly known of since the middle ages, in which each number is the sum of the preceeding two numbers. Le Corbusier's progression used the ratio of 1 to 1.618 otherwise known as the golden section. Le Corbusier attributes great significance to the fact that this proportioning system can be derived from the ratios of the major parts of the human body. Thus for Le Corbusier not just the proportions but also the actual numbers of his series have fundamental symbolic significance. "The numbers of the Modulor are ... facts in themselves, they have a concrete body." (Le Corbusier 1951). Le Corbusier was convinced that man would be somehow more content if the environment around him were proportioned symbolically to echo his own form. This then brings us to our fourth and final group of constraints used as design generators, the symbolic constraints.

Symbolic constraints are likely to have the greatest influence in the explicitly expressive and communicative design fields such as graphic and stage design. Paul Rand (1970) writing about graphic design tells us that: "It is in symbolic, visual terms that the designer ultimately realises his perceptions and experiences; and it is in a world of symbols that man lives. The symbol is thus the common language between artist and spectator." Rand stresses that the task of the graphic designer is only incidentally to produce a "good layout" in formal terms. The design idea is not produced simply by shuffling the elements into a pleasing arrangement. For Rand the graphic designer's central task is to find the essential meaning in his material and then to abstract and symbolise. Many writers refer to the process of distilling the symbol down to its simplest form. Richard Buckle (1955) explains how the ballet designer Sophie Fedorovitch "believed in cutting down the decor and dresses of a ballet to the minimum". Describing her set for "Nocturne" for example Buckle tells us how "she only used a few pillars stuck with posters, framing a ground-row and a well-lit sky cloth yet we knew we were on the Butte Monmartre, with Paris sleeping below". Sophie Fedorovitch's process began not with representational drawings on paper but by collecting a few pieces of material and pinning together to explore the mood and atmosphere which was to be achieved.

The symbolic properties for the formal visual materials, mass, colour, texture, proportion and so on is in itself a subject too vast and complex to be considered here except in the most brief and superficial way. Unfortunately much of the literature in this field is, like Le Corbusier's work, full of rather fanciful and largely unsubstantiated assertions. Alexander (1959) has argued that the real value of proportioning systems lies in the sense of order they impart to any construction rather than from the symbolic significance of the golden number. Experiments have certainly shown that we do tend to judge rectangles based on the golden section to be pleasing to the eye but on the other hand few people are actually capable of accurately distinguishing golden rectangles from similar rectangles. No doubt the argument will continue.

That the human perceptual system drives us both to seek and find meaning in the environment about us is certainly beyond dispute. Thus we find pictures in the clouds and the coals of the fire almost as readily as we recognise the faces of our friends and relatives. Whether environmental symbols are universal, cultural or just personal is less easily established. It is easy to assume that commonly accepted symbolic connotations are more fundamental that is in fact the case. Thus black is a western sign of mourning but in other cultures the widow may even wear white. Smith (1974) has argued that our perception of meaning in the environment is closely linked to the mechanisms of the brain. In particular he has stressed the importance of the more primitive part of the human nervous system. "The limbic brain not only exists but seems to contain circuitry which generates a psychological appetite for symbolic references going right back to archetypal origins." The link suggested here between the frontiers of modern neuropsychology and traditional aesthetic criticism is perhaps rather tenuous but the subject matter is clearly vital. We do react to massive cathedrals or medieval city centres in the way that Smith describes. Such environmental images are full of meaning, for whatever reason, and it is therefore right that designers should think positively about the meaning their work will have for others. Norberg-Schulz (1975) has warned of the dangers of architects attending only to formal constraints. "Spatial structure is not a goal in itself, but is only relevant if it concretises the spatial implications of a character...." Norberg-Schulz's approach to meaning in architecture is based less on psychological mechanisms and more on cultural patterns than Smith's, and he identifies the crisis facing the modern designer as resulting from the pluralism of values accepted in modern western society. The unambiguous stable religious and social standards of previous ages no longer structure our perceptions of the existential meanings of the man-made world. Today

11.8 The form of Sydney Opera House was generated by symbolic intentions, and many of the practical constraints were not considered until much later in the design process

anything goes, and there are no longer even strictly observed rules of fashion and dress previously used to symbolise our respective social roles.

We have seen that all constraints whatever their function, radical, practical, formal or symbolic can be used as generators of form. How they are actually used, in what sequence and with what emphasis is what differentiates one designer from another. It is at this point that both the writer and reader of this book should proceed with caution. Naturally each of us have our preferences and obsessions. Some may be more fascinated by formal geometry while others are concerned with the more expressive content of their work. Some are clearly best at dealing with practical problems while others may feel that only the radical issues should be allowed to dominate. There is surely room for all these kinds of designer. As a result of their different interests the solutions they design will probably solve different sets of problems and their work will thus appeal to some observers and not to others. It is for example well recognised that there is such a thing as "architects' architecture", and a Design Centre award will not guarantee the sales of a new product.

This writer then must be careful not to endorse any one approach more than the others. It seems likely that, since each particular design situation has its own characteristics, the most important constraints will vary as much from problem to problem as interests vary from designer to designer. The reader should take care not to narrow his interests and thus form too rigid a design strategy unless he intends to specialise in a very limited way. We saw something of the way problems can vary in chapter six in a brief look at the way housing problems tend to present similar internal constraints but varying external constraints. Similarly some problems may present relatively simple radical constraints but complex practical ones while others may be primarily a matter of symbolic content. It is also true that design problems are to some extent at least what one makes them. To return to our earlier example of Utzon's design for the Sydney Opera House it is fairly obvious that not only did this designer initially concentrate on external rather than internal constraints but also on symbolic and formal rather than radical or practical constraints. How the building will eventually be assessed as an auditorium for music remains to be seen. Its excellence as a landmark of international significance is beyond question.

At this point we should just examine the importance of the concept of constraints. It may not always be obvious that what is important to a client or a user is not always critical during the design process. In Agabani's study of the way architectural students perceive design problems one experiment required pairs of students to design a children's nursery. After reading the brief and watching a video recording of the site the students were themselves recorded as they discussed the problem. The very first recorded comment from one pair of subjects was to the effect that: "the most important thing is that we are going to have children playing outside." Now while playing outside is certainly a requirement for nursery design it hardly seems to be "the most important thing". However the same designer continued: "so which way round do you put all the playing areas so that they can wander around?" This can now be seen as an assessment not of what is most important to the client or user but what is critical to the designer. In this case orientation of major spaces towards the protected and sunny side of the site followed by a consideration of vehicular access was quite fundamental in organising the overall form.

In a recent study of how various groups of users responded to a new university building it was apparent that the users' and designers' perceptions of the problem had been quite markedly different. (Lawson and Spencer 1978). The users by and large thought the architects had done a good job in solving what they saw as the difficult problem of satisfying the esoteric environmental needs of a complex research and teaching department. The architects however had not seen the demands of the academics in such a critical light. For them the problem had largely been one of a difficult site where road noise, foundations and the possibility of future extension determined the overall building form. The constraints which are critical to the designer are thus those which have the widest influence on the physical form of the solution. As we have seen they are as likely to be practical issues as much as radical ones. Unless communication between designer and client is unusually good the client may never even be aware of which constraints dominated the form of the solution. The designer's role in relation to a client who wishes to be closely involved in the design process is therefore necessarily very much a teaching one. It is easy to see how, in the absence of such an interaction between client and designer, the design process can appear quite mystical.

So far we have seen how both empirical research and the anecdotal evidence gathered from practising designers suggest that the early phases of design are often characterised by what we might call analysis through synthesis. The problem is studied not in minute detail but in a fairly rough way as the designer tries to identify not the most important (to the client) issues but the most critical in determining form. Once a solution idea can be formulated, however nebulous it may be, it can be checked against other more detailed problems. In the experimental studies mentioned earlier both Eastman's and Agabani's results show the combined use of evolutionary and revolutionary modifications of early solutions. In the evolutionary phase the designer is really following his nose, gradually modifying the embryonic design as it is tested to see if it satisfies constraints and is found wanting. Eventually unless the design proves totally successful one of two things happen to halt this evolutionary phase. Either the general form of the solution reveals itself incapable of solving enough problems, or so many modifications have to be made that the idea behind the solution is lost and abandoned. In either case the designer is likely to choose the revolutionary step of starting a completely new train of thought.

This is the point where creativity is required rather than ingenuity. The train of thought is broken and no longer sequential. Some effort has to be made to look for a new set of problems or a new angle. This brings us as close as we can get so far to the centre of design thinking, for the way in which the designer chooses to shift his attention from one part of the problem to another really constitutes his design strategy. In experimental studies we have observed many variations. Some designers only shift attention when they come to a dead end, while others seem to deal with several ideas in parallel. Some designers delay their first sketchy ideas of a solution for longer than others, and thus perhaps combine more constraints in their first attempt. Perhaps most importantly some designers are much more willing to abandon partially developed solutions than others. As yet we can say very little about the desirability or otherwise of any of these traits. Perhaps in the future we shall be able to discover more of the way in which good designers control their strategy.

This book does not conclude that one kind of design strategy is better than another. Indeed it does not even teach or set out complete strategies, and it certainly does not recommend that professional designers should consciously observe and monitor their strategies. The way attention is shifted from one part of design problems to another is best left a matter of experience and judgement until such time as empirical work gathers evidence to the contrary. At the beginning of the book we saw how highly developed physical skills such as playing golf or the flute can be taken apart and broken down into elements which can then be examined separately. We concluded then that no talented golfer or professional flautist could possibly play in the highly self-conscious way suggested by the tutors quoted. So it is with design, but bad habits can usually be acquired more easily than good ones. The golfer can lose his swing and his game, and may need to return to the elemental approach he used as a novice.

In this book we have taken apart the design process to identify the elements, as seen by this author, which can be recombined in many ways to form many design strategies. In the unselfconscious mode such a strategy is based on the experience and judgement of the designer and is used to switch attention between parts of the increasingly clearly defined problem and the emerging solution. Such a process resembles the "executive" hypothesised by the cognitive theorists discussed in chapter eight; and it forms the central pivot of the mental act of design. In chapter nine we saw the importance of the ability to shift the context of our perceptions upon the creative process. Creativity depends upon being able to see the same thing or idea in several different ways, the ability to generate a variety of perspectives.

The model of design problems developed in chapter six has generated a framework for much of the discussion in this chapter and it also offers a framework for both the evaluation and development of design strategies. The student of design can use this model as it stands, modified to suit his own needs, or better still he may devise his own model. The model is not important in itself but rather for the opportunities it creates for giving new directions to design thought. As a design tutor, the author constantly finds students who are chasing their own thoughts around in small circles covering only a narrow section of the whole problem. As designers we often waste time banging our heads against brick walls because we have become obsessed with some particular issue which later on in retrospect is seen as unimportant or is perhaps even of our own making. Design usually has to be practised in a limited period of time. We do not seek the perfect solution, not even the right solution but as good an answer as we can get in the time available. It is therefore vital to develop a strategy that allows for the widest possible search of the problem. The model of design constraints can be used as a crude form of checklist to assist in this search.

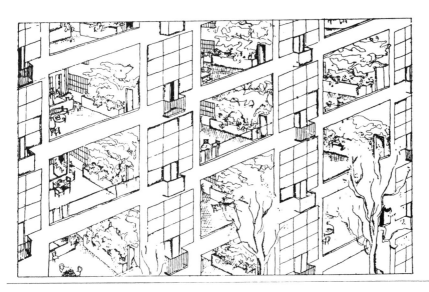

11.9 Le Corbusier's Modulor, a formal method of generating building geometry

12 Design tactics and traps

Part of the art of dealing with wicked problems is in the act of not knowing too early which type of solution to apply.

Rittel and Webber, *Dilemmas in a General Theory of Planning*

... that sudden fits of inadvertancy will surprise vigilance, slight avocations will seduce attention, and casual eclipses of the mind will darken learning; and that the writer shall often in vain trace his memory at the moment of need, for that which yesterday he knew with intuitive readiness, and which will come uncalled into his thoughts tomorrow.

Samuel Johnson, *Dictionary of the English Language*

In this chapter we shall not so much be considering grand philosophies or even overall design strategies but rather the detailed mental tactics of design. There is thus nothing intellectually demanding about the contents of this chapter, which really deals with some techniques which can be used to control the direction of thought when attacking design problems. Since we have already rejected the notion that there is only one path or route through the design process there is no way that the ideas in this chapter can be presented in a "correct" sequence. Instead the reader should regard the mental techniques reviewed here as a bag of tricks which may be delved into as seems appropriate by the designer at the time. There have already been a number of books written which describe design techniques. Frequently such techniques are not complete methods for designing but rather ways of getting through particular parts of the design process. Unfortunately standard definitions have not yet been agreed in this field and quite minor techniques for tasks such as problem identification, user research or solution evaluation often appear alongside attempts at much more comprehensive aids to design and the whole collection is described as "design methods". In fact there have been relatively few true design methods as such which provide guidance through the whole design process, and it is probably less misleading to describe the contents of many books on design method simply as techniques. So long as the reader does not expect too much from these tools and is prepared to adapt them they may well prove useful. A good selection can be found in Jones and Thornley (1963), Jones (1970) and Cross and Roy (1975).

Here we shall concentrate more on the business of organising and controlling the mind rather than prescribing methods of working. Thus the ideas given here more closely resemble the prompts and suggestions a director might offer his actors than a full script. All the tactics discussed here are in reality simple tricks of the trade for manipulating attention. A physical analogy is probably helpful here in appreciating the role of attention in design. For a designer beginning to work on a new problem it is rather as if he were an explorer freshly awoken to find himself in a strange forest. To begin with he has no real idea where he is. How large is the forest and what shape is it? Where then should he begin searching and how? In essence what the designer would like is a map showing how one part of his forest relates to all the others. The great advantage of a map is that it allows us to "see" the whole forest at once. Unfortunately, from inside the forest it is not so easy to get a reliable picture. What you see depends upon such factors as where you are standing, which direction you are looking in and your depth of focus. The explorer of the forest may not initially be able to see very much from where he stands; and he may have little idea which way to go. Sometimes it may help to climb a tree in the hope of getting a better view but it is not always easy to get sufficiently high to see over nearby trees. A good view might be gained from a clearing or on a hill and the intelligent explorer will first look for such vantage points. Alternatively a road or pathway, river or stream may not only offer a view but possibly suggest in which direction our explorer may search. Thus with a few carefully chosen vantage points the explorer may be able to sketch out a rough map of the forest which he can use to find his way around while filling in more detail.

In order to find his vantage points the explorer uses some very general model of the way forests are laid out. He may know which species of tree are the highest or easiest to climb. He knows that a water course will flow from high to low ground. He may know something of the habitat chosen by animals or birds and be able to read their tracks and so on. So the clever explorer does not just blunder about aimlessly but rather uses his knowledge of forests in general to guide his search for key features. So it is with design. The designer too has a very general idea of the way design problems are composed. The experienced designer can use this model to help him decide where he should start searching. The model of design problems developed in this book may be used in just this way. To begin with there is probably little to be gained from climbing several trees in the same part of the forest, and the designer probably wants to identify a fairly wide range of constraints before exploring any group in detail.

The designer is on the horns of a dilemma in that he cannot expect to arrive at an integral synthesis of all the needs of a problem until he has a comprehensive grasp of the constraints. On the other hand he is unlikely to appreciate many of the constraints until he begins to propose solutions. Initially the real secret of good designing lies in how to begin searching the forest as it were, so as to piece the whole together. The designer is always on the lookout for ways of simplifying or subdividing the problem in order to make his task more manageable, but there are many pitfalls or traps for the unwary here. We shall next explore some of the more common design traps and discuss ways of avoiding them.

The category trap

The most obvious and attractive trap for the unwary designer is the tendency to categorise the problem in solution terms before it has really been studied. Good solutions to design problems are the result of an integrated synthesis and can thus be intellectually as well as visually satisfying. Solutions are attractive, memorable and easily recorded by means of drawings, models or photographs. We see design solutions around us every day but we rarely stop to ask ourselves exactly what were the problems they solved, and indeed we may often remain quite ignorant of the real difficulties encountered by their designers. We may admire the stage set revealed by that most theatrical of all moments, the withdrawing of the curtain, and we may applaud the designer, but how much more impressed we would be if we knew just what problems he had concealed. The technical problems of manufacturing the set, the difficulties of striking and setting the stage during the performance, providing satisfactory acoustics, concealing the lighting and many more such problems are often known only to the designer himself.

Architects in particular suffer from the ignorant critic. Even other professionals can seldom appreciate the true nature of an architectural problem simply by viewing the solution. Conflicting demands from within the client organisation, the remoteness of the user, difficulties with the bearing capacity of the soil, an unsympathetic planning authority, changing circumstances during the design period, restricted or inflexible methods of financing the scheme, insufficient time allowed, and many many more difficulties remain inscrutable to all but the most perceptive and insightful of architectural critics.

However, in spite of this knowledge, we continue to make our own implicit assumptions about the nature of design problems. We see a building which attracts us either in real life, or more often these days in the pages of a journal. We make our assumptions about the problems it solves and later, when faced with an apparently similar problem we make the connection with the previously remembered solution. Sometimes this disease can become so acute an affliction that design students seem more to be searching for problems to fit their solutions than the other way about! Indeed we tend to classify design more by types of solutions, which are easily recognised and categorised rather than by the problems which gave rise to those solutions. In fact these categories seem to refer to the quintessential purpose, or in terms of our model of design problems, the radical constraints. Thus we refer to architects who specialise in housing, educational, health and welfare buildings, offices, theatres and so on. Table O of the SFB classification system operates in exactly this way.

But all this is rather misleading since the radical constraints only form a part of the total problem. Housing does pose quite a different problem to theatre design for instance, not just because "living" is different to "theatre going" as an activity but because the legislative controls are quite different. Office design may be different to school design as a result not just of the activities but also because a private client is quite unlike a public client. Hospitals are different to residential buildings in that the practical constraints imposed by the need for elaborate service systems are much more problematic. Conserving old buildings or building in urban areas will require more attention to be devoted to the external constraints than designing a new building on a green field site.

Thus the model of constraints can initially be used as a crude map to search for the vantage or starting points most likely to open up the major or central issues. Later the model can also be used as a way of deliberately transporting the designer to another part of the forest. Many of the so-called creativity techniques are generalised methods of provoking the mind into looking at a problem from new viewpoints. The designer who seems stuck, or in a rut, can analyse his thoughts to discover where in the model of design constraints he has been concentrating his efforts. A deliberate shift to consider constraints which are different in function, domain or generator should raise new issues allowing different problems to be identified and promoting a fresh train of thought. Perhaps the main role of the tutor in design schools is to inject enough new ideas into the student's mind to precipitate this change of perspective. While the student concentrates on his design however, he may miss the important lesson which is that he must learn not to rely upon a tutor but to be able to explore the problem for himself.

It is interesting that one of the most notable attempts to produce a design technique for problem identification has grown out of a situation where there is little student-tutor contact. The Problem Identification Game, or PIG as it is called for short, was devised by Reg Talbot and Robin Jacques for an Open University course on "Man-made Futures". The ideas behind PIG are in essence very simple, sensible and valuable although they have been rather unfortunately obscured by the unnecessarily elaborate rules of the game which uses a galaxy of boards, cards, dice, charts and stickers! The basic idea of PIG is that the designer first distills the problem down to a very short and simple statement. From this statement the designer identifies a crucial problematic relationship called in the jargon of the game a "Key Problem Pair". The problem is then explored by generating a succession of further problem pairs using simple stimulus techniques selected at random. Thus, to use one of the examples from the manual, many of the difficulties experienced in the post-war housing programme can be summarised by the primitive statement: "slum clearance can bring disadvantage to slum dwellers". The technique requires only pairs of elements in problematic relationships to be listed with the relationship itself ommitted. So this now becomes "slum clearance — slum dwellers". This very crude oversimplified statement is next amplified by randomly selecting a series of well known devices for shifting the context of perception. The five devices or mental tricks employed are: "conflict", "contradiction", "complication", "chance" and "similarity".

"Conflict" requires the designer to convert his elements into interested parties who might be viewed as in conflict. Thus our example can become: "Town planners see a need for change and renewal not necessarily felt by the aged who have lived in an area all their lives." From this the designer now generates a new problem pair: "Town planners — aged residents". Using either of his problem pairs the designer can now employ another device such as "contradiction" which relies upon trying to contradict an earlier statement of the problem so as to see another side of the issue. For example: "On the other hand it is the aged who most need the benefits of modern safety standards and conveniences" could become "Slums – safety and hygiene".

The use of the "complication" device might now lead us to realise that the benefits are not quite so simple and that "Modernisation complicates the tenants' lives by increasing their rents"; a statement which in turn becomes "modernisation – tenants income". The "chance" device quite simply depends upon finding a word at random from a dictionary or a newspaper to provoke a new relationship. When trying this out the author found the word "softly" which, perhaps because he was listening to music, made him think of a piano. This in turn raised the problem that many old people have often collected large and cumbersome furniture or carpets and curtains which may not easily fit into homes designed to modern space standards so that not only do the subjects of slum clearance lose their old homes but also their belongings. This might become "new designs – old furniture".

Finally PIG uses the device of looking for "similarity" which is the age old trick of gaining understanding by using analogy. The bulldozer is to houses rather as the plough is to fields. The gain of dealing with the whole area at once is offset by the fact that the existing pattern of streets or hedgerows, and thus the whole character of the place, is lost. Such thoughts could lead to the problem pair "economy of scale – existing community".

The use of such simple techniques and the deliberate search of the problem by using the model of design constraints should enable any designer to uncover some key vantage points from which to study the rest of the problem. For most designers this process probably becomes progressively less selfconscious. However it is probably always a sensible precaution to do at least some deliberate and highly selfconscious problem identification in order to avoid too narrow and blinkered a view.

The puzzle trap

Design problems are not in themselves puzzles. In a puzzle the elements are defined, objectives are clearly stated and there is usually one correct, or at least optimal, solution. As we saw in chapter 7 design problems are not so clear cut, but it is often possible to find pseudo-puzzles within design problems. Such pseudo-puzzles may be constructional as when trying to form a junction between a number of members such as posts, beams and roof trusses which all come together at one point. There may also be planning puzzles such as how to arrange furniture in a space or spaces within a volume. These puzzles,

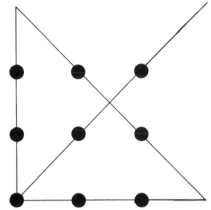

12.1 The nine dot – four line problem. Join all the dots with only four straight lines without lifting the pen from the paper

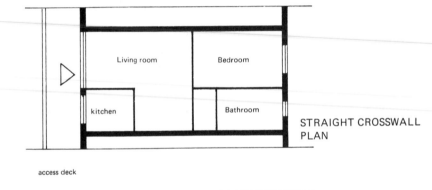

STRAIGHT CROSSWALL PLAN

access deck

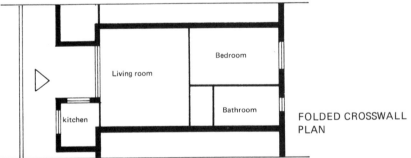

FOLDED CROSSWALL PLAN

12.2 What is the narrowest acceptable bay width for terrace houses? It depends on whether you assume the cross-walls must be straight or not

even though they form part of a much wider design problem can often offer all the irresistible mental temptations of brainteasers. For many of us it can be very difficult to forget such puzzles until they have been solved. The crossword and the jig-saw can be very compulsive, and such is the attention they demand that we may find ourselves mentally returning to that unsolved clue while we should really be concentrating on something else altogether. This type of mental activity is performed purely for its own sake. There is no need to question the worth, relevance or practical value of such puzzles. We do them purely for the satisfaction of meeting a challenge. Of course it is necessary that the correct answer is usually recognisable when it appears in order for us to experience the sense of achievement and reward.

Designers also rely upon this obsessional devotion to a problem to provide the mental drive to achieve their goals. However there are some dangers in treating the pseudo-puzzles which can be discovered in design problems as if they were no more than brain-teasers. Firstly the designer may be trapped into thinking that the elements and rules of his puzzle were given and unquestionable. In fact many brain-teasers rely upon the solver himself implicitly taking an over-rigid view of the rules. The famous nine-dot four-line problem is a case in point. The solver is asked to cross all nine dots with only four straight lines (drawn without lifting pen from paper). Most early attempts to solve this problem show an implicit adherence to the unspecified rule that no line may go beyond the perimeter of the square defined by the dots. Once the thinker identifies this rule as part of his thinking and rejects it, the puzzle is easily solved.

In design pseudo-puzzles can easily be created by fixing a limited number of constraints and puzzling out the consequences. Such a technique is undoubtedly an excellent way of getting to grips with a problem so long as the designer remembers that the original assumptions, which defined the puzzle, were of his own making and are therefore open to question later. A simple example of getting caught in this trap was provided by a group of architectural students working on a public sector housing scheme. They were in the usual situation of trying to decide how many homes of differing sizes they should fit onto the site to achieve the most socially desirable pattern and to satisfy local housing need while still obtaining an overall density and mix which would attract the most economical sums from the legislation governing cost allowances. Eventually the students had defined a puzzle as being how to fit single-bedroom deck-access flats onto a part of the site unsuitable for single or two storey dwellings. After several days of puzzling out a plan for the flats they were unhappy with the shape of the living room which they felt would be dark and depressing. During discussions some of the rules of the puzzle which they had implicitly defined began to emerge as follows:

1 The structure to be load-bearing cross-walls carrying concrete plank floors
2 All rooms to have natural ventilation
3 Kitchen to be a separate space from the living room
4 Internal circulation to be kept to a minimum
5 Living rooms to overlook access deck and face south

The students were naturally trying to get as many flats as possible into a given length of deck and had reasoned that the bathroom and bedroom must face away from the deck. They had calculated the minimum possible spacing of the load-bearing cross-walls as the sum of the minimum acceptable widths of the bathroom and bedroom. Because all this and much more besides had been reasoned so logically the students had come to regard some of the less explicit rules as just as inviolable. One of these unspoken, and thus unquestioned, rules was that the cross wall must be straight. Once this was recognised a much more acceptable solution emerged very quickly. By staggering the kitchen partially in front of the next dwelling the living room could become a more flexible shape and shallower without increasing the overall width of the dwelling. Although slightly more expensive this

12.3 Fit these jig-saw pieces together into the simplest shape

12.4   The second jig-saw

solution also gave a small semi-private external space off the access deck which encouraged a sense of identity and broke down the public corridor feel of the access deck, and so was judged to be worth the cost. Thus one of the most useful ways of avoiding the puzzle trap is to analyse and evaluate your own implicit rules or boundaries.

The puzzle trap can still be dangerous even if the designer successfully solves his puzzle, for it is then that he is most likely to feel a sense of achievement and reward which are easily transferred to a pride in the solution. Unfortunately, good solutions to pseudo-puzzles can often become problems later on. The whole point of defining a pseudo-puzzle is to narrow down the problem and thus generate a nicely contained and packaged sub-problem which is small enough to be tackled in its entirety. Thus the designer who defines pseudo-problems is really behaving in a way similar to that advocated in Alexander's famous method in which design problems were decomposed into clusters which were then analysed and solved independently. However the difficulties are quite likely to occur when the designer tries to combine the solutions to all his pseudo-puzzles.

To illustrate this try the two jig-saw puzzles shown in the diagrams. The object is to fit the pieces together into the simplest possible form. Undoubtedly the best answers are a square and a rectangle which can be achieved as shown. If you discovered solutions for yourself you

12.5 Solution to the first jig-saw

12.6 Solution to the second jig-saw

probably experienced slight feelings of pride and satisfaction which may even have extended into a desire to show the solutions, which concretise your wit and ingenuity to friends and colleagues. The next and much more difficult part of the problem however is to fit all the pieces from both jig-saws together. In fact the real obstacle to success is the existence of the earlier solutions. This part of the puzzle can be solved much more satisfactorily by abandoning the two earlier solutions and recombining the pieces as shown.

The design student can often be found struggling with this second phase. He is clearly pleased with the solutions to earlier pseudo-puzzles and reluctant to abandon them and consequently is really trying to solve yet another pseudo-puzzle this time entirely of his own manufacture. Architecture students tackling housing problems for the first time often generate house type designs which, while being excellent in themselves,

12.7 Solution to the complete puzzle

do not allow for a flexible pattern of combinations on site. Regrettably this is also to be seen in many real post-war housing schemes in which terraces of houses or individual dwellings are littered around the site with unusable and largely indefensible areas of ground between.

There is nothing wrong with defining and solving pseudo-puzzles in design. Often such a technique is the best way to make rapid progress and develop a better understanding of the problem and possible solution options. The trap lies in forgetting that the puzzle was artificially contrived and can therefore just as easily be challenged to make even further progress.

The number trap

Little needs to be said here about the number trap since it is so dangerous that we have already devoted a whole chapter to it. Chapter 5 on "measurement, criteria and judgement in design" explores the dangers associated with the indiscriminate use of numbers. If a problem can be reduced to numbers then we may operate upon those numbers with all manner of mathematical tricks. Of all the problem-solving languages available to us, mathematics is undoubtedly the most powerful, and therefore the most dangerous when misapplied. It is easy to tell if one number is larger than another and therefore whether one solution is better than another if their performance can be described numerically. Unfortunately it is rare for us to be able to describe every aspect of performance numerically and it is in this simple fact that the danger lies.

For example a larger room is obviously more desirable than a smaller room, all other things being equal. Regrettably the "other things" are not always equal and therefore simply measuring the size of a room and relying upon this as some sort of criterion of success can be not only misleading but, as we shall see, actually self defeating. The illustrations, kindly provided by Geoff Jones of Building and Urban Design Associates in Birmingham, show how these designers proposed to arrange a double bedroom in a conversion of existing houses to flats. The local authority measured the area of the proposed bedroom and refused planning permission on the grounds that this bedroom was some 0.086 square metres below their criterion of 12.5 square metres for main double bedrooms. The designers were therefore forced to enlarge the room by making structural alterations and therefore incurring considerable expenditure. What is most interesting here however is not that the second solution was no better, but that it was actually worse since the amount of usable space was effectively reduced!

Designers can be just as guilty as officialdom of falling into the number trap. Architectural students will often treat the areas of rooms as absolute even though it can often be cheaper to provide larger spaces when, for example, the external skin of the building can be made shorter by eliminating re-entrant corners, or because two spaces could be adjusted to be the same size thus simplifying the structure.

It is very difficult to defeat an argument based on the use of numbers, unless you can also substantiate your case numerically. Many architects must, like the author, have been confronted with an engineer who advises on a more efficient system of providing heating or structural support, or with a Quantity Surveyor who can show how savings can be made in the capital cost of the design. The task of then explaining to the client that, there are other considerations which are not easily quantified but may be essential to the quality of the place being designed, offers one of the most severe tests of the architect's advocacy skills. However his task may become much easier if he forgets the burning issues of

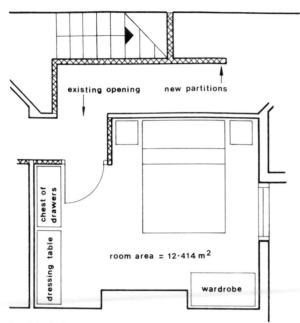

existing opening   new partitions

chest of drawers

dressing table

room area = 12·414 m^2

wardrobe

1 original plan : pre - planning dept

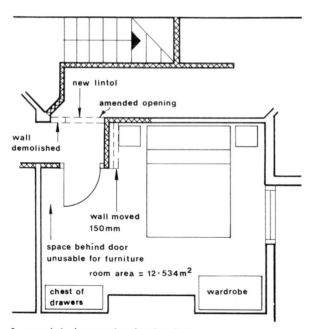

new lintol

amended opening

wall
demolished

wall moved
150 mm

space behind door
unusable for furniture

room area = 12·534 m^2

chest of
drawers

wardrobe

2 amended plan : post - planning dept

12.8   Does the extra 0.12 sq metres insisted upon by the planning authority improve the design?

quality and instead demonstrates how, for example, although capital costs are reduced by the suggested changes the running or servicing costs would be increased, or perhaps, how much more expensive it would be to extend the building later.

None of this should be taken as a criticism of numerical problem solving techniques per se. Wherever numbers can be meaningfully used mathematics, however simple or advanced, is likely to offer the most reliable decision-making language. The designer however should always be on the look out for the number trap by always asking what kind of numerical system is being used and how the values were arrived at. If he does not he can become mentally trapped by the power of numbers; a trap which in turn often leads to a puzzle when misdemeanour is compounded by felony!

The icon trap

We have already observed how, as designing became professionalised and separated from making, designers came to rely not upon manipulating the actual solution itself but rather some iconic representation of it usually in the form of drawings or models. We also discussed in Chapter 2 how this gave the designer what Jones (1970) calls a "greater perceptual span". That is, he could see all his design at once and thus consider major alterations by changing the drawing or model. Drawings and models are iconic, in that they resemble the real object they portray in a visual way. Unlike the word "Cat", which is a symbolic rather than an iconic representation, a drawing of a cat actually looks to some extent like the real thing and we do not need to learn a language to appreciate its meaning. Because drawings and models are so direct and apparently simple to read it is easy to forget that they are very limited in their ability to represent the real world.

It is relatively easy to see potential failures by studying design drawings if you know what to look for, and these failures need not just be restricted to visual appearance. Any practised architect can, by studying working drawings and using his experience, tell whether a detail is likely to exclude the weather, prove difficult for the builder to construct, produce staining of the materials and so on. However none of these failures are actually apparent in the drawing itself. The architect is relying upon having met a similar situation to that described by the drawing before either in theory or practice, and upon knowing how well it worked. It is generally much easier to gain this necessary feedback for physical performance than for performance in use, and so it is consequently much more difficult to detect failures due to such factors as insufficient privacy or social isolation, when looking at drawings.

But we can easily get even more careless when seduced by the power of drawings. It does not take long for design students to develop the ability to imagine three-dimensional form and space from two-dimensional drawings such as plans and sections. Often however their confidence in their own ability is rather misplaced and tutors find that students have begun only to draw a few key drawings such as plans. They will tell you with innocent confidence that they know how the elevations and sections look. If it is difficult to spot potential failures in drawings, then success in detecting those failures in imaginary drawings is even less likely, and these overconfident design students are well on the way to being caught firmly in the icon trap.

It is clear then that designers do not just use drawings to communicate with clients, builders or legislators. Drawings are an essential part of the design process itself. A process, which it has already been suggested, in which problems emerge along with solutions rather than entirely in advance of them. Eastman (1970) in his study, already described, in which subjects were asked to redesign a bathroom, showed how the problems considered by designers were, to some extent at least, a function of the drawings they produced. Thus those subjects who worked exclusively in plan and omitted to draw a section failed to think about such problems as whether small children could reach taps on the wash basin. Problems involving the vertical dimension, Eastman found, were much more likely to be considered by those subjects who drew sections. Similarly, a common error amongst architectural and interior design students is the failure to ensure adequate headroom over staircases, particularly when inside irregular spaces such as are to be found under pitched roofs.

The trouble then with two-dimensional drawings such as plans, elevations, and sections is that while they only show a small part of the overall picture, they can often appear to be much more comprehensive. The designer must deliberately take the trouble to "see" two adjacent elevations as just around the corner from each other before he can be sure that he knows how a corner will look. The use of three-dimensional drawings such as perspectives or axonometrics is thus most desirable; a point every design tutor quickly wearies of making to his students, but even this has its pitfalls. Designers can, with only the most minor error of draughtsmanship, deceive themselves as to the real size of spaces or objects unless they measure their perspectives. Unfortunately the mechanical setting up of measured perspectives is usually not found to be conducive to the free flow of thought in the early stages of design.

The three-dimensional model is thought by many to provide the highest level of iconic reality. Here too though there are dangers. If the scale is very small as in architectural design then the viewpoint is unreal and can lead to buildings designed to be looked at from high-flying aircraft. Wehrli (1968) in his experiments asked subjects to design schools using block models. He found a tendency to establish symmetry either in part or all of the design, even where it was most unlikely to be perceived on the ground had the real building been constructed. Wehrli also showed how this symmetry was much more likely to be formed about the axis running forwards away from the designer than about an axis at right angles to his line of vision. The axes of the drawing board, T square and set square can dominate thought even more dramatically.

Drawings and models then can impose their own grammar on the designer's thought processes and the visually sensitive designer can often be lead into problems of two or three dimensional composition that exist in the drawing only. The spatially able designer may also find abstract drawings insidiously taking on spatial meaning. The author recalls a three-dimensional net which he constructed to explore and explain the desired relationship in his thesis design as a final year architectural student. Metal rings representing different functions were connected by different coloured cottons to show the necessary connections for the various groups of building users, mechanical services, vehicular access and so on. During a criticism it became apparent that one of the tutors had already "seen" this model as representing a building constructed in a doughnut arrangement around an internal lightwell. For him this image was too powerful and real to allow further meaningful discussion of the model as it was intended.

Great care then, must be taken to avoid the icon trap. The simple message here is that the more icons, whether they be drawings or models, that are used the less likely is it that any one will take over. Drawings and models should also be viewed from as many different angles as possible. Turning a plan through 90° or looking at it in a mirror is surprisingly effective in developing new perceptions and ideas. Those who doubt the power of such a simple trick should look at a close friend's face in the mirror to see just how different it can look!

The image trap

The designer then is always working with some sort of mental image of the reality of his designs. Until the building or object is constructed no-one really knows just what it will be like to live in, look at or hold. The

12.9 "Streets in the air"?

designer tries to create and manipulate his own "reality" and may use drawings and models to help in this process. However the designer's mental image usually contains many qualitative ideas too nebulous for iconic representation. These ideas are often expressed as symbolic images, and although these symbolic images are undoubtedly essential to the designer he can easily become trapped by his own illusion. Symbolic images are much more difficult to check than iconic representations since they are less concrete and open to much greater variations of subjective interpretation.

An example of this symbolic image building can be found in descriptions of the designs for the now famous Park Hill flats in Sheffield. The multi-storey structural system, subsequently used again at Hyde Park and Kelvin was described by its architects as having a "street" form of access. Jack Lynn (1962) argued that the tradition then growing up around Le Corbusier's L'Unite d'Habitation was inappropriate to the English Culture. Le Corbusier's ideas he argued had to be understood in the context of the traditional French apartment building with one common entrance hall controlled by a concierge. By contrast "centuries of peace and a hundred years of housing reform in this country had given us the open street approachable from either end and off which every house was entered directly through its own front door". Lynn argued that the continental indoor form of access was an "ambiguous space, being neither private nor public, and as such can make a positive contribution neither to the life of the individual nor to the social life of the community".

Another of the architects of Park Hill, Ivor Smith (1967) tells us how the designers thought "there seemed to be some quality of the open air that was liberating, whereas enclosure seemed to be inhibiting". Lynn is rather less direct, preferring to pose rhetorical questions: "Does gregariousness depend on the open air? Why is there so little conversation in the tube trains and in lifts? Are there sociable and anti-social forms of access to housing?" All this is used to set the scene and create an image which enables us to see the high level open-sided access decks of Park Hill not as "corridors" but as "streets". "Streets" have been loaded with a positive image of fresh open-air and sociability while "corridors" are neutral, inhibiting and ambiguous. The image is extended by reference to the refuse shutes as the "modern equivalent of the village pump".

The reality of the Park Hill "streets" today is perhaps rather less romantic. Due to the sloping site the "streets" only connect with the ground at one end. For the rest of their length they may only be reached by stairs or lifts. The "streets" serve flats at levels below and above as well as at the street level, and are not overlooked by any windows save for the obscured glass panel in the veritable battery of front doors. It is thus difficult even to see the physical resemblance to a traditional Sheffield street, let alone the social resemblance so imaginitively described by the architects. In fact the image of "streets in the air" can, and did, become so powerful that we failed to notice some discrepancies between image and reality. Only relatively recently for example, has any quantity of deck access housing been built in Sheffield with living spaces actually overlooking the decks so that the residents can see their neighbours come and go as on the traditional street.

These comments should not be taken to represent criticism of the architects involved. The image of "streets in the air" undoubtedly facilitated some of the most memorable and progressive housing built in this country. Without such images designers will never be able to attempt new solution forms, but any designer must surely be permitted, as must his critics, to revise his ideas when the image has actually been realised. It is all too easy for a critic to pour scorn upon a design when he has the unfair advantage of examining the reality. As we have observed earlier the designer, unlike the scientist, does not seem to have the "right to be wrong". Hard though this may be on designers it is only by this successive process of realisation and criticism that we increase the accuracy of designers' predictions.

While the designers of new forms should perhaps be allowed to indulge in speculative image-making, this technique can often be used to disguise the commonplace or familiar and thus mislead us into believing that in someway the design will be free of the disadvantages normally associated with previous similar solutions. Such deception is a most dangerous, and all too common practice. It is, however, often possible to break free of this image trap by concentrating on the individual words used to describe a design, rather than the apparent overall meaning.

Sometimes image-building is so obvious and is so expected that we learn to interpret and to translate the words to give a more realistic impression. Thus the estate agents' description of the "stone built detached period cottage having superb scenic views of the rural country side and offering an opportunity for sensitive renovation and modernisation," may be interpreted by the cynical house hunter as an "old dilapidated and rather isolated house". Much though they may scorn these commercial images, designers can sometimes be just as guilty of deceit. In fact their guilt is rather greater since they often deceive even themselves. I once had to listen to an architectural student describing how his housing scheme was organised to keep pedestrians and cars separated. The cars he said would drive into a kind of "mews court" surrounded by the dwellings which looked out over open ground. The "mews court" he told us would be "treated with soft landscaping and provide space for visitors to park their cars, give access to the residents' garages and create a space where the enthusiast could tinker with his car, and allow access for delivery vans". The sketch showed a leafy and sunny view complete with a lady carrying a parasol being escorted across cobbles to a vintage car by a man wearing plus fours, a cap and gauntlet gloves. The students' tutors were rather suspicious. We asked if he had checked on the turning circles of the delivery vehicles; he had not. We wondered how he would protect the trees from damage caused by games of football; he thought the children would play elsewhere. We asked if he had checked his scheme on a heliodon to see just how much sunlight would actually penetrate the court; he had not thought that necessary. We asked if he had any idea how much more the cobbles would cost to lay than tarmacadam. He did not know, nor was he sure what he would save on to find the extra money out of the limited budget available. We suggested that the residents of such housing might be more likely to own old bangers than beautiful vintage Bentleys. He did not think that would matter; so we asked why he had drawn the Bentley. He was of course a victim of his own image. By the simple device of calling a garage court a "mews" he had managed to load it with connotations of a more gentile age and a more expansive life style. Thankfully in this case only the designer himself was fooled, but such was the power of his image that it is doubtful if even the built reality of yet another dirty, noisy and barren garage court would have broken the spell!

Positive or attractive images then can be created merely by the calculated or careless use of "plus-words" like "mews-court", "street" or "village pump". The technique relies upon our ability to conjure up a generalised image in our "mind's eye". Characteristically such images have much more to do with atmosphere than with detail. We only have to call a new satellite housing development a "village" rather than an "estate" and thus evoke all the pleasant associations already established in our minds with villages. Vandalism and social problems may happen on housing estates but villages are well adjusted and stable communities, goes the insidious mental argument and we are caught firmly in the image trap. Once in the trap the designer may no longer look to see just how his new design may differ from a traditional village or how a high level deck may differ from a street, and thus his mind becomes closed to large areas of the problem.

Plus-words are very much a matter of fashion. Recently architectural students have been fond of vernacular allusions. Thus anything to do with the traditional forms of construction can be used as a plus-word, materials such as "brick" or "slate", forms such as "pitched roofs", building types such as "barns", or more abstract concepts such as "small-scale" or "domestic" all carry positive connotations. All this can be seen as a reaction to the previous fashion for a "machine-aesthetic" based on the brutalist and functionalist tenets of the modern movement. Then to describe a design as "logical", "functional" or "structurally honest", was to pre-empt and side step all criticism. I well remember one of my design tutors explaining to me how it was not "honest" to use a laminate imitation of wood, but acceptable to use wood veneers themselves. Even when another tutor showed him a real wood veneer so highly polished that it was indistinguishable from a plastic laminate he remained unmoved. "Honesty", he maintained, "was everything".

13 Designing with others
Cedric Green

Our language can be seen as an ancient city: a maze of little streets and squares, of old and new houses, and of houses with additions from various periods; and this surrounded by a multitude of new boroughs with straight regular streets and uniform houses.

Ludwig Wittgenstein, *Philosophical Investigations*

... a fusion of psychological and social modes of explanation is long overdue. ... British psychologists still tend to ... assume that the causes of behaviour lie within the organism: while anthropoligists and sociologists take it for granted that the roots of a human's actions are to be found in the rules and expectations of the social order that surrounds him.

Liam Hudson, *Frames of mind*

Like almost all skills which involve the whole brain in thinking and making value judgements, designing is not something that one begins to learn from a certain age (on entering a design school), or stops learning a while later (on qualifying). It is quite unlike motor skills – driving a car or playing a sport – in that it requires the integrated exercise of a broad range of vaguely defined abilities like reasoning, analysis, synthesis, communication, valuation, categorisation, aesthetic judgement, sympathy, moral judgement and so on, all of which are developed rapidly through childhood and early education, and more slowly after that. (Green 1971). The only motor skill that might be associated with design is drawing if the designer's products are primarily visual, but it is also quite possible for a good designer to be a bad draughtsman.

In one way learning to design is like learning a language. Everyone is a designer in a small way and the ability is picked up naturally from childhood without conscious effort. Every child draws and arranges things and begins to order his or her own little world in a way that might be called designing. This skill becomes, like the use of language, gradually more fluent and capable of ordering larger collections of things, and for most non-professional designers it culminates in the ability to design the complete arrangement of furniture and possessions in a house and create a personal environment in harmony with our own family needs and as an expression of one or more personalities. That, when you think about it, is no mean feat of design, and some people are better at it than others even without any design training, just as some people speak and write more fluently and eloquently without ever having studied their language or literature.

This aspect of design – as a kind of language or communication – is going to be emphasised in this chapter. For we do not only speak to each other in words and gestures, but also with things. The shapes, colours and arrangements of things that make up the environment speak of the ideas, values and dreams of their designers in a way that nearly every one can grow to understand. We speak of incoherent design, eloquent arrangements, clearly articulated forms and much of the terminology of criticism in design and literature is interchangeable.

An enormous amount of research has been done on how children acquire language but very little on how they acquire natural design skills. But the similarities mean that some of the conclusions about language learning can be transferred and give us an insight into design learning.

The first thing to remember is that language and communication is meaningless without other people with whom to communicate. Despite the theory that is growing in acceptance now that there is a genetically transmitted predisposition to language – a latent knowledge of deep structure of grammar common to all languages (Chomsky 1968) – children only learn with others such as parents and other children who are speaking and playing with them. Children who have survived and grown up in the wild with wolves or other animals have not shown the ability to use language and do not use toys or play games with them. But even in the most primitive human societies, the games children play can be seen to be part of a social learning process – imitating and practising the actions of adults that are perceived to be important and interesting (Roberts 1959). They play with each other with symbols or tokens of the things that adults seem to value, copying actions and attitudes that are observed, creating a world in microcosm and even where playing alone, filling their world with substitutes for people – dolls and imaginary beings.

Children's games do not subdivide the world into academic categories like "language" and "design", but weave everything together in a unity of imaginative play. The way that things can stand for other things is particularly striking − a block can be a house or an elephant or a satellite − in the same easy way in which language can provide a word, a particular sound, to stand for something else, as long as everyone playing the game agrees to it. In the restricted context of the children's game particular allocations of meaning can be agreed just as nonsense words are invented and used in a code that often baffles adults. Children's drawings are like that too: adults make squiggly shapes on paper and give them names of things, so young children do the same, only their shapes are halfway between representation and words − they stand for the things in the way the blocks in the games did and they tell a story. Drawings are a child's way of writing.

It is this use of drawings that makes the most direct link between language learning and design learning. In the undifferentiated experience of childhood everything is woven together, drawings and words, representations and symbols, functions and meanings, and only gradually are things put into categories and separated. But during that intensely creative phase when children acquire the basic command of their language, they are at the same time learning to structure and order shapes, on paper, in space, and make connections between their environment and their games with words and things.

Later on language is differentiated from other "subjects" and its learning formalized; "design" continues to be learned in a rather diffused way; part of it becomes "art", some "craft", bits of it come into all kinds of activity like drama, hobbies, domestic science and so on, and the basic skill continues to be developed unselfconsciously, rather in the same way that one unselfconsciously learns to speak and write grammatically and eloquently without ever having had a lesson in formal grammar. During this period, the social context is very important. We need other people to speak with in order to learn a language, and techniques of second language learning are recognising this increasingly. It is conversation and communication in the language that builds unselfconscious fluency. The same is true of design. Remember that the word "design" is being used here with the emphasis on "meaning" in the special sense of "meaningful ordering of things in an environment" and although problem-solving cannot be clearly separated from this, it relates to it in the same way that the special language of mathematics and logic relates to the language of conversation and communication.

Design learning after childhood is a matter of understanding the meanings that other people ascribe to the things that make up their environment, and experimenting with relationships between them. The most obvious example is in clothing and fashion. Quite small children are very aware of the clothes and styles worn by their friends and those they admire. Often in the same way they are intensely conservative about fashion, needing to belong to a group and express their membership by the design of clothing and of other personal artifacts like jewelry, or possessions like skateboards or other toys that are displayed publicly. Adults too are conscious of the meaning and symbolic value of the things which surround them. However much we may deplore it, most people who have not been "taught" about design are more conscious of symbolic values than of values like "fitness to purpose" or "honesty to materials" and are motivated to acquire things by the feeling that those things are consistent with their place in the social group to which they belong (or wish to belong). Even the people who surround themselves with "well designed" things may be motivated more by this than by a totally rational belief in objective "good design". Fashions change in good design even in the Design Centre, although perhaps not as fast as they do in the High Street Shops.

To understand design as a social process it is necessary to see it in the context of the way every individual is conscious of design and in a small way is a designer of his or her own environment. In the same way, Wittgenstein showed that to have an understanding of the special language of logic or mathematics one had to go back to ordinary language of everyday communication (1956). He used the metaphor of a "language game" to illuminate the nature of verbal communication as a transaction between individuals. Design even more clearly can be shown to resemble a game, and has even been rigorously analysed using mathematical game theory (Green 1973); that analysis is too esoteric for our purpose here but it is worth considering the relationships in the design game in some detail. Apart from the light the metaphor of a game can throw on our understanding of design, there is another and more directly relevant reason — that is because specially designed games can be used for specifically educational purposes to provide an experience and environment in which aspects of design skill may be learned.

Games are a very old means of resolving conflicts which might, if allowed to develop into hostilities in other forms be much more destructive. Competitiveness, aggression and unco-operative behaviour of all kinds can be channelled into a risk-free simulation of the situations that in real life might be intolerable if the participants acted without inhibition. Most people recognise this aspect of the playing of games as widely different as squash and Diplomacy. But games only work as a means of resolving the simulated conflict, if the framework of rules is accepted by the players. Implicit in this rule structure are the values of the society or group who accept them. The fraternity of chess players values logical strategic thinking in situations of relative certainty, whereas poker players value the ability to assess probabilities in situations of great uncertainty, and take risks in a show of apparent confidence. Games in general are a reflection of the way that we should like our real conflicts to be resolved. And conversely games are a means of dramatising and communicating the values of certain kinds of behaviour. They are a subversive method in the moral education of individuals.

As has already been pointed out, creating something for oneself in private, involving no one else at any stage, is an activity which we are more likely to call "art" or self expression than design. The moment the product has to satisfy requirements imposed by others an element of "design" creeps in and it is this characteristic that we are using as a basic distinguishing feature of designing. The original element, that of personal expression, does not disappear, and it is this that creates all the interesting problems and makes the field of design so rich and fascinating. For no creative individual can be so altruistic, so devoted to the solution of others' problems, so committed to satisfying others' needs and desires, that he denies himself any self-expression or recognition in his work. It is certainly true that some people have advocated this in design, but even if it were psychologically possible it would probably not be socially desirable for it would result in a grey uniformity of "good design" stripped of any individuality, quirks of personal expression or appeal to individual customers or users who themselves are looking for an expressive environment. In fact there is a complex transaction going on, through the design process, between different and competing expressions and all the functional and technical needs that must be satisfied. Often what may be seen as not expressive at all to one person, becomes to others powerfully symbolic and expressive of an attitude, a style, a set of values that they hold. Take for example the design of the Jeep. In contrast with the "styling" and selfconscious expression of American car design it may originally have seemed totally functional and lacking in any style. But it has continued to be produced and imitated in designs like that of the Mini Moke, right up to the present, and used for purposes quite unlike those for which it was conceived. Mechanically, the modern successors of the original jeep are very different and yet important aspects of appearance like headlights, grille, mudguards and overall lines are recognisably similar. Possession of a jeep "style" vehicle now symbolises a sort of trendy rejection of many values implicit in consumer oriented design, and, more positively, may imply alternative values as well as being purely utilitarian. The history of design shows this process happening over and over again. The success or survival of a design is bound up with the associations which it provokes, what it may come in time to symbolise, and with shifts in social values or buying power of groups in society who have the power to stimulate production or repetition of the design.

No designer can produce something which is expressionless or purely functional. And the first thing that anything he designs will express is himself – his own unconscious preoccupations, bias, limitations, experience, values and personality. As he develops his language of design, in other words, settles on a vocabulary of forms or types of solution and a manner in which he repeatedly uses them, the products of his work will become recognisably associated with him (or his office or group).

Used in this way the word "expression" does not have quite the same sense as when it is often used in art to mean "communication of emotion or feeling". Rather it is a more elusive kind of expression, which cannot be consciously achieved, but which develops quite naturally in time. It develops at a number of levels: first as a personal expression, then later when out of the designer's control it can become an expression of something else, like the Jeep, adopted by a sector of society for its collective symbolic purposes. Products of design go on, long after they have been produced, being transformed both in material and in meaning, in an evolutionary process of selection and adaptation, survival and final extinction.

If we think of an individual designer faced with a commission or task, the problem seems, on the face of it, quite simple. Someone (we will call him a "client") needs something made that serves a number of requirements that might be quite mundane and easily stated. As we have seen though, there may be unstated needs that are more complex, and it is the job of the designer to ferret these out and try to make them explicit. But on the other hand the designer has his own needs which are not the same as those of the client, and could in fact be in conflict with them. If he wants to succeed as a professional designer he must win approval for his designs not just with that client, but with a wider circle, in a way that will attract more clients or advance his career in some other way. The first and most obvious group whose approval a designer seeks are his fellow professionals, through publication, prizes, and building up recognition of the particular quality of his designs. Now, even in a period that has been dominated by the ideal of functionalism, it is true to say that, in professional circles, good design is recognised by criteria that go beyond pure functional performance. In fact, acclaimed designs are often relative failures in their functional performance and the method of assessment almost never takes into account whether the client or users were satisfied. The values placed by the designer's own subculture are far more likely to be on visual or expressive qualities or the "meaning" that the design has. The dominant professional milieu in which the designer finds himself will determine the kind of thing he is trying to express through the design, while at the same time he is solving the client's problem.

An example which illustrates this very vividly is the concern for energy conservation in design. This may seem on the face of it, to be a purely functional consideration, but it is not as simple as that. It is basically a moral issue – a feeling that, for the sake of future generations, we ought to be conserving our non-renewable resources. A design that is seen to be doing this implies values and has a meaning that goes far beyond function. All too often, the symbolic gesture is taken to be enough, and questions are not asked about the cost of making the gesture, or what sacrifices the client is having to make for it. At the time of writing, the most widespread expression of concern for energy consumption is the appearance of water solar collectors on buildings. The cost in resources like copper, energy in production and capital, for this symbolic gesture are far greater than the energy savings will justify compared with insulation. But insulation is usually invisible and cannot be used as an expression. Of course the client may share the designer's desire to express moral values of this kind through the design and may be delighted at professional acclaim for the thing he commissioned but not at the expense of his needs. If his needs were only mundane physical things like performance and accommodation there need be no conflict, but the truth is that very often the client needs the design to express something about himself or his organisation – power or prestige or a certain kind of taste. Not every designer may be able to reconcile his own values, aspirations and expression with those of a particular client with divergent needs. The professional ideal of service to his client may allow him to suppress his own needs, or he may enter a complex relationship with the client which is in many ways like a game. Almost every designer/client relationship goes through the "game" stage: it is a process whose purpose is to resolve potential conflicts and to settle in advance what is to be the balance of objectives that the designer will seek to achieve. It begins with an explicit understanding between the parties about the rules, the "moves" and the "rewards" and then a series of actions (the moves) within the rules in which each acts either co-operatively or competitively to achieve the goal – a design, the payment of fees or a pat on the back.

The moves in this game are those actions or decisions that each party takes on his own and then presents to the other: first the client's decision to appoint the designer and present him with a more or less vaguely defined brief; next the designer's interpretation of that in terms of a tentative design or a more detailed statement of requirements; then the client's response to that – changes to it, or more clearly expressed desires; then a more detailed design; and so on, until both parties are satisfied or the commission is abandoned. Each move can be seen as a process of elimination. At each action or design, more alternatives are excluded until only one out of the almost infinite number of design possibilities existing before the first move, has been chosen. This outcome will be one that both parties might not have been able to envisage or predict at the beginning. Like the exact arrangement of the final pieces on a chess board when a game is concluded, it is a unique consequence of the preceding moves, but unlike the chess game, it is the unique consequence, not the playing of the game that is the goal. Every design game should end in a mutually satisfying "draw". A "win" for one party means either that the design does not get carried out if the client "loses" and does not like the result, or that the design is unsatisfactory from the designer's point of view. Of course one may be cynical and say that the designer's only goal is usually the fee, and although this may be true in very many cases, such a view reduces the role of the designer to that of a technician, and ignores the independent criteria by which the designer's own subculture judge "good design".

It is important to appreciate that co-operation in this process is an important ingredient, just as it is in many team games. Competition may be there too, but it is often the stimulus to co-operation. So far we have just considered a basic two-person game, but in fact it is rarely that for long. The design must be approved by someone else, other than the client – a planning authority, or a marketing organisation, or a financial backer – it must be produced and parts of it must have specialist design work done. Altogether it must satisfy and meet the needs of a great many people other than its sponsor and its designer. Classical game theory shows that games with more than two persons inevitably lead to coalitions between players and therefore co-operation to achieve mutually beneficial goals (Rapoport 1960). But coalitions are usually provoked by third parties whose goals are in conflict with those of the coalition. So a designer and his client may find that in order to win planning approval, they must resolve their differences to enter a coalition against a planning authority. Or with equal frequency the client and planning authority may successfully overcome the designer's goals, or designer and planning authority defeat the client's and permit the production of a design that is good in the eyes of conservationists and design critics, while not being entirely what the client wanted.

Behind each one of these roles stands a complete subculture with its own values and attitudes to design, and a person belonging to it acts both as an individual and as a representative of it, to varying degrees, according to personality and in response to the people with whom the game is being played out. So, despite the behaviour that might be predicted by an analysis of roles, goals and likely coalition formation, an individual may be motivated by extremes of altruism and co-operative tendencies or conversely by selfishness and competitiveness, that overcome the normal social pressures that come to bear in the "rational" game. This happens frequently enough to make the outcome of design games quite unpredictable, so there is no hope of using game theory to determine the outcome in particular cases. But the game-like nature of the process makes it possible to simulate it for the purposes of education and sometimes as a preliminary in the real design process.

Design games for education

The rapid growth in the use of gaming-simulation techniques has been in response to what was seen as a failure in the traditional educational systems, particularly those which purported to be vocational. The failure was in bridging the gap between theory and practice. As theory became more abstract and was taught in ways which were less easy to relate to the activities to which they referred, practice became dominated by the minutiae and details of execution and management, and the processes in which the practitioners were caught up became too big and complex to understand clearly.

The earliest examples of this were in military training, and the Prussian military academy was simulating battles by means of role playing war games with elaborate models as early as the mid-19th century. Since the 2nd world war, and stimulated by Van Neumann and Morgenstern's classic explorations of game theory (1949), every field of practical human activity which has some theoretical background has felt the impact of gaming-simulation techniques. It has been most appropriate in its application to fields where there are a lot of decision makers working inside a socio-economic system in which their decisions may have physical consequences: Marketing, Business, Administration, Politics, Planning, Engineering, and now more recently

Architecture and Design, have been explored using gaming-simulation models.

Game theory and gaming simulation are a part of General Systems Theory although strictly speaking gaming simulation has no theory, just a body of examples. It is a technique which borrows methods and terminology from a lot of related disciplines in the social sciences and tries to unify them under that vaguest of terms, "games".

In education, gaming simulation sets out to achieve a number of simple goals: to demonstrate to students the structure and "mechanics" of the system in question by means of dynamic "models" of the interpersonal relationships, the roles and their definitions, the physical, economic or quantifiable components and the rules and relationships which limit their behaviour: to allow students to experiment with modes of behaviour towards each other within the system, to experience the effect of personal attitudes and values on the behaviour of others and so on the physical system itself: to permit individuals or groups to experiment with strategies or tactics to attempt to discover their effect in the system, in a "risk-free" context rather than making real mistakes with possibly disastrous consequences. This last goal is the most debatable one, because it involves an element of prediction, and only in systems with a very deterministic physical basis and a minimum of scope for the unpredictability of interpersonal human reactions in reaching decisions can one hope for useful results. All these goals can be achieved by actual practical experience, but only slowly and sometimes by making mistakes with real consequences. But sometimes, without a mental model of the whole system beforehand, a student will find it very hard to understand.

Gaming simulation does something else perhaps better than any other educational technique. By providing a vivid and often enjoyable exercise for the participants, and by the fact that it seems so relevant and presents so much complexity, it motivates them to greater interest in the subject and leads to studies and explorations which are far more valuable than the exercise itself. For example, students often are inspired to go on to try to design a game themselves, from which far more will be learned than just playing a game.

The first games used in a design school were probably the ones designed by John Rae for students at Hornsey College of Art in 1966 (Rae 1967). They were solely concerned with communication patterns in groups solving problems and were not specifically related to the needs of designers. Planning and land use games like CLUG (Cornell Land Use Game) were developed in the United States and found their way

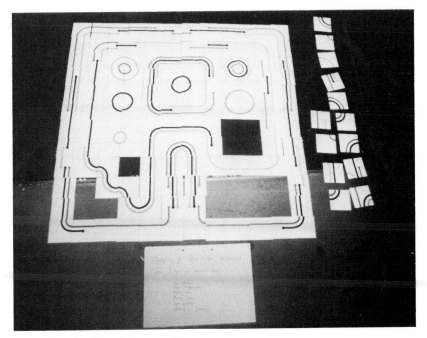

13.1   Results of a typical game of JOIN

into a few UK schools of architecture in the late 1960's. The first game that was devised specifically for designers was JOIN, produced and used at Cheltenham College of Art in 1969 (Green 1977). He used a children's game designed by Ken Garland and produced by Galt Toys called CONNECT as the basic kit, but with rules which simulated the processes of group design of a "product" that had to meet various physical and cost requirements. JOIN led on to the production of GAMBIT, a building design game. In it, teams of up to 5 players competed against each other to produce a building design, using a magnetic tile planning system. The design can be simply evaluated to determine its cost, thermal loss and gain, heating running cost, structure, massing, and their interactions. Each player in a team takes a specialist role and teams compete to produce designs to meet particular goals.

One of the many things that these games try to achieve is the integration of thinking about technical aspects with consideration of form and more subjective aesthetic matters. Students learning to design often find that the curriculum in a design course separates these aspects; technical matters are taught by specialists in a way that is often inimical to their integration in project work which consequently becomes an

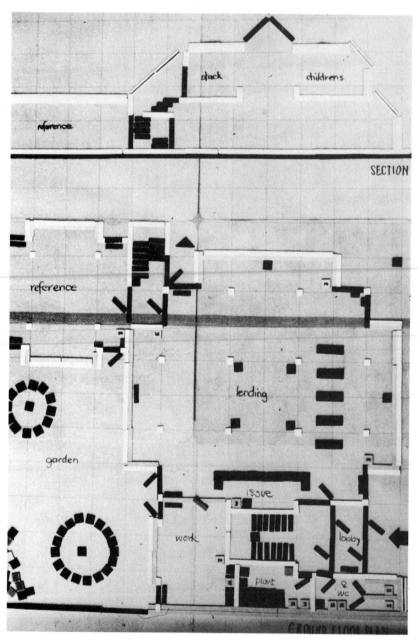

13.2   Plan and section of a small branch library produced by a game of GAMBIT

exercise in styling. GAMBIT, by emphasising the group process in integrated designing, conveys to the students both the advantages of collective work in design and some of the difficulties. No designer in the

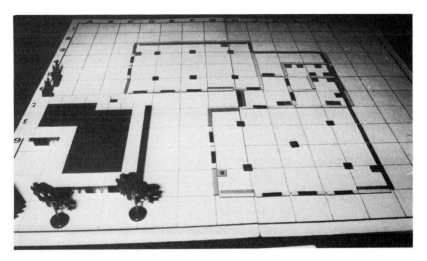

13.3 Plan and block model of a classroom block after GAMBIT

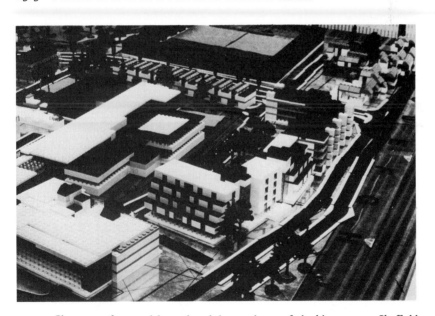

13.4 Close-up of a model produced by students of Architecture at Sheffield University playing URBISM on a local area

modern world can completely master every specialist technical skill involved in producing a complete design and so the use of specialists is inescapable. But on the other hand, a good design is not produced by just putting together a diverse group of specialists and letting them get on with it. The process, to work well, involves the individuals building

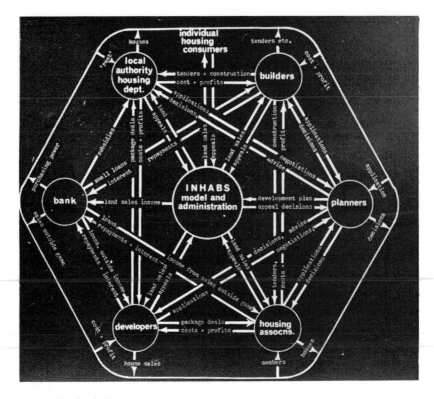

13.5   Graph of roles and relationships in INHABS

up a rapport between them, understanding each other's view-point and being able to communicate well. Perhaps this is something that cannot be taught or artificially stimulated, but at least a student may be able to recognise its absence and understand why there is a need for it. GAMBIT attempts to do this by making the success of the result depend clearly on the successful integration of roles and rapport between the players. It stimulates an appreciation of the degree that the design of something complex like a building is a collective process, depending on language and communication of values and ideas.

These same objectives underlie the use of gaming simulation exercises at a larger scale − in urban design. INHABS (Instructional Housing and Building Simulation) is a very highly formalised model of the process of housing design concentrating on economics, lay out and building form. The roles and relationships between them are shown in the diagram. Out of this has grown another game, URBISM (Urban Instructional Simulation and Method) which is a "free game", that is, a relatively unstructured role-playing simulation of a particular real urban

13.6   Model of a portion of Broomhill after an URBISM game based on a 5th year architectural course project

situation, which the students have studied. Each game becomes structured by its players according to their perception and understanding of the real situation they are simulating. The result, like INHABS, is a very large model made with small plastic blocks (Lego) of the physical results of the decisions and designs made by the players. It has often been suggested that if the real planners, politicians, developers, architects, public representatives, press, landowners and other interested parties all involved in negotiations about the development of, or change to, particular areas in cities, could get together to play URBISM or other urban simulation games, it would be extremely revealing and might anticipate and neutralise conflicts which in reality are extremely damaging and usually caused by difficulties of communication and understanding of values (Green 1974).

From childhood onward it is now being appreciated that games have a very important educational function. With a few exceptions, what is learned from playing games is to do with how one relates to other people. Designing, as distinct from free artistic self-expression, is a social process. It takes place between individuals who have particular roles that they have chosen to play in society. But there is an element of individual self expression in the way that role players interpret how they should act which introduces conflict into their relationships and makes the outcome – the design – a result of their resolution. If every participant in the design process agreed about the goals and about how they should relate and act then the social aspects of the process could be described, formalised, and organised by a bureaucratic procedure. Luckily perhaps that is not possible in a society which values individuality and the freedom to give it some expression. So the process of design of almost everything in our environment can be understood by the metaphor of a game, and learned by simulating the process in design games.

14 Designing with computers

The change from thinking about machine design to thinking about systems design is not a gradual evolution but a discontinuity; an abrupt change in basic philosophy comparable to the change which occurred when the engineer took over design problems from the blacksmith and carpenter.

W. T. Singleton, *Man-Machine Systems*

In 1968 one could read all existing literature in English on the subject of "artificial intelligence" within one month. Now it takes about six months.

Nicholos Negroponte (1975), *Soft Architecture Machines*

Computer-aided design is no longer a new idea. Ever since computing power became commercially available there have been those who have sought to define a role for computers in the design process. Until relatively recently however computers have comprised large and extremely expensive systems which were complex to operate and maintain, and consequently their use has been restricted to well-funded research institutions and other large organisations. The advent of the new micro-processor technology has brought computing within the grasp of the domestic scale, casual user, and at the time of writing this book we have not yet fully understood the implications of the techno-social revolution which some forecast will result from this change. However it is already apparent that computers may be expected to play an increasingly important role in the design process and this may well influence the way designers think. Not all writers feel this to be a change for the better. (Cross 1977). We shall therefore briefly examine the nature of artificial intelligence, its advantages and problems.

There is not space here for a comprehensive coverage of computers and computer-aided design systems, and the interested reader is recommended to read Mitchell's (1978) thorough treatise on the subject, but a brief description is necessary. In dealing with computers it is useful to distinguish between the concepts of "hardware" and "software". The hardware of a computer consists of the information processing circuitry itself, the memory banks for storing information and the various peripheral devices for the input and output of that information. By contrast, the software comprises the sequence of instructions given to the computer to enable it to perform all the desired exchanges and transformations of information. Computer software includes not only the particular program in use but also all the back-up systems resident in the machine which allow for the input, editing, translating and running of such a program.

Since the early generations of computers there have been considerable developments both in terms of hardware and software. We have already noted how the micro-processor has revolutionised the information processor and memory banks of the computer by cramming them into a domestic priced, desk-top box. The peripheral devices too have become very much more sophisticated. Of particular interest to designers are the graphical devices such as cathode ray storage tubes and digitising plotters which can directly input and output drawings. Micro-processors are now increasingly being linked to mass-produced colour television sets to reduce costs even further, and dramatically increase availability.

The advances in software are much less apparent but no less dramatic than the new hardware. Computer programs are ultimately converted into a series of binary numbers which can be easily stored inside the computer. The binary counting system has a base of two instead of the normal base of ten used in decimal numbers. Thus "11" represents eleven in decimal (10 + 1) and three in binary (2 + 1). The higher level programming languages such as Fortran, Basic and Algol allow the writer to use decimal numbers, conventional mathematical operators and a range of instruction words. Obviously the computer needs an extensive dictionary and grammar, called a compiler, to translate this near-human language into machine language. Even the smallest and cheapest desk top micro-processor computers now usually have such a facility "wired in" enabling them instantly to translate "Basic" programs. The last generation of mini-computers were seldom capable of supporting such sophisticated software without large additional memory banks.

Modern computing power is small, easily maintained, cheap and much more easily operated than the previous generations of computers. As a result of all this development the limits to computer potential in design are no longer set by the technical system but rather by our ability to discover ways of developing useful applications programs. We are no

14.1(a),(b) Two of the micro-processor based graphic computing systems

longer hampered by the need to provide huge, expensive, air-conditioned computer rooms or by crude mechanical input and output devices but rather by our own limited appreciation of the problems of combining human and artificial intelligence in one decision making system.

Some appear to argue (e.g. Cross 1977) that computers are intrinsically harmful to such a decision-making process. Certainly some of their arguments should raise issues of great concern to design theorists. Will designers feel intimidated and inhibited by the computer? Will the sheer pace and speed of the computer automatically generate a stressful experience for a designer who, as we have already seen, needs to indulge in a certain amount of semi-conscious and even unconscious cerebration? Will the necessary reliance on numerical methods in computing distort the emphasis of design?

Such questions can all too easily be posed in a rhetorical manner. The computer today has a generally bad public image. We tend to blame the computer when served with an inaccurate fuel bill, or when our driving license is delayed for several months. Of course, the reality of the situation is that these unwelcome quirks of computerised systems are more usually the result of a human failure to predict the particular circumstances in which the machine would appear to act erroneously. Any computer system is only as good as the program which is written by the all too human systems designers. Clearly there is much evidence around of bad or incompetent design of computer systems. Whether or not a computer should be used in a particular situation is therefore not a question we can answer in an absolute and static way. The success of a computerised process is a function not just of the characteristics of computers but also of our ability to understand the process which we are attempting to computerise. Since we understand so little about the design process it may therefore seem rather foolhardy to attempt a computer-aided design process, but there is a nice paradox here. The application of computer techniques to any system forces us to make explicit otherwise implicit procedures, and drives us to examine and investigate our assumptions about the way in which we make decisions. Thus whatever the ultimate value of computer-aided design systems their very development is quite likely to teach us more about designing itself, and for this reason alone computer-aided design research should be encouraged and studied by designers.

Attitudes towards computer-aided design tend to be as polarised as attitudes towards computers in general. A great number of the rather more generalised and theoretical contributions to the literature in this field seem to be based more on belief than on hard evidence. For example Cross (1978) criticises Maver's work at ABACUS to establish computer-aided architectural design systems, not so much in terms of the work itself but more in terms of its use in practice. "The examples he (Maver) gives of successful CAD applications are for buildings such as district general hospitals, comprehensive schools and airport terminals. These are all apparently necessary features of living in the modern world – big, centralised, impersonal institutions." Such a quotation may be compared with the statements of writers such as Negroponte (1970) who tells us that: "our interest is simply to preface and encourage a machine intelligence that stimulates a design for the good life and will allow for a full set of self-improving methods. We are talking about a symbiosis that is a cohabitation of two intelligent species." The reader is left to decide to what extent these two writers have fallen into the "image trap". Clearly the use of computers in design is influenced not just by the nature and capabilities of computers but by generalised attitudes towards modern technology which form philosophies parallel to those discussed in chapter 10.

Research into computer-aided design has been extremely varied in nature. Some workers have concentrated on simply trying to automate what they see as a recognisable and describable element of a design process such as calculating the size of a building element. Other workers have tried to build complete computer-aided design processes, and others still have simply speculated and tried to explore the future. We shall next briefly discuss some examples of each approach in order to discover something of the advantages and disadvantages of working with computers and how this might influence the way designers think.

One might reasonably expect that computers would initially be most readily absorbed in those areas of design which are already fairly dependent on numerical techniques, and indeed this is just what has happened. For example Logcher et al (1967) had developed their Integrated Civil Engineering System (ICES) and incorporated a designer-oriented language for structural engineers (STRUDL) to use the system long before comparably sophisticated architectural applications had been comtemplated. On the same basis the computer soon invaded other areas of design amenable to numerical techniques such as the aerodynamic shaping of aircraft and car bodies or the sizing and organisation of lift systems in buildings. However when computers were introduced into areas not traditionally treated by numerical methods computer-aided design became much more controversial.

One such controversial application was to the problem of planning *derived from the computer*

	superinten-dent room 54	male staff and rest room 44	changing room 43		work room and clean supply 46	47	48		
medical store 55	entrance 42	nurses station 41	38	35		sterile supply rm 45	nurses changing and rest room 49	50	
medical staff change 40	medical staff rest 39	anaesthetic room no 2 37	36	anaesthetic room no 1 33	34	sisters changing and rest room 51	52		
	18	17	2	3	11	12	53		
	general theatre-1		ante-space		general theatre-2				
	15	13	1	4	7	9			
	16	14	6	scrub-up 5	8	10	32		
	sterilising room 24	22	sink room 19	20	25	emergency theatre 28	30		
	23	21	small theatre 27	26	29	31			

14.2 Whitehead and Eldars' program requires the user to input the number of journeys between any two spaces and then it designs the building to minimise the total travelling time within the building

buildings so as to minimise the travelling time of people circulating between spaces. A classic example of this technique was published by Whitehead and Eldars in 1974. They demonstrated the effectiveness of their program by designing a hospital operating theatre suite. They argued that the time wasted by hospital staff moving around such a building could be costed by relating it to the salaries of the various groups such as surgeons and nurses. The input to the program is thus a series of numbers representing the expected number of journeys made between each pair of spaces for each group of hospital staff over a unit period of time. These figures are weighted by the relative salaries and the computer then seeks to minimise the distances between the pairs of rooms generating the greatest circulation. In fact the computer proceeds simply by first positioning the room with the largest overall circulation figure and then adds the room which most relates to it, continuing on to

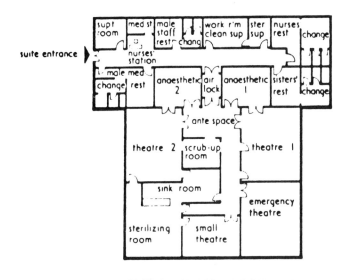

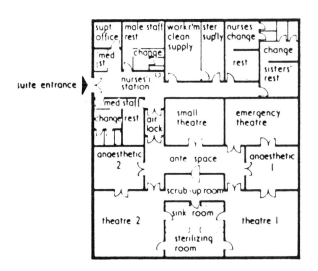

14.3 The output from the Whitehead and Eldars program must undergo several stages of manual transformation before it becomes a buildable plan

position each successive room so as to minimise the circulation to all existing rooms.

Such a technique is open to many criticisms. First it does not produce an optimal solution. Cross (1977) showed that some designers were able to produce less expensive solutions (in terms of circulation cost) although the average human performance in his experiments was actually worse than the computer program. The second major criticism of the Whitehead and Eldars approach is that the program depends for its input upon data that is in reality less precise than it appears. The patterns of use of buildings are in fact quite difficult to predict as accurately as is required to produce the interaction matrix which forms the input data. People do, to some extent at least, respond to their environment and therefore, unless a building is to be identical to one already in use we cannot be absolutely sure what the circulation pattern will be. Such patterns are also quite likely to change with time and circumstance, as are the salaries of staff! However these criticisms would also apply to a human designer's efforts were he to attempt the same objective of minimising circulation.

The third criticism is perhaps the most serious for the proponents of computer-aided design, and that concerns the way in which such a technique impinges upon the designer's own thought processes. When he has run the Whitehead and Eldars type of program the designer is left with a quasi-optimal solution in terms of circulation costs. Of course there are many more issues which influence planning, some of which are more quantifiable than others. Capital and maintenance costs tend to be minimised by reducing the perimeter wall. The external constraints include problems of access, view, privacy, lighting and solar gain which all contribute to the disposition of spaces. The practical constraints of structure and construction and the distribution of services all suggest building configurations which may not be sympathetic to the solution derived by the computer. The crux of this difficulty is that the computer has removed one set of internal, client/user oriented constraints, namely circulation, and ignored all the other complexities of the problem. The designer therefore is now faced with the problem of modifying the solution to suit all these other requirements; he is thus seen to be reacting to a situation presented by the computer which has rather dominated the process. Whether or not the use of such a technique would really assist in producing a better building overall, or in making it easier to design a better building is therefore far from clear.

Thus we can see that so long as computer-aided design was restricted to the design of relatively simple objects such as glass bottles or even complex objects with clearly defined parameters such as boat hulls then computer synthesis was both feasible and showed benefits of reliability and speed. However when the problem is more multi-dimensional as in building design, simply isolating one issue and optimising will not necessarily be helpful. One way around this difficulty is to be even more ambitious by programming the computer with the rules of the game in terms of other constraints. For example the practical constraints of the structure and construction of buildings seem to be fairly explicit and logical and therefore amenable to such treatment, but so far the explicit logical description of building construction has proved to be something of a mirage. In reality there are so many different materials, techniques and options available to the architect that it is impossible to map out all the alternatives. In fact we recognise that the design of structure and construction is as much of a creative act as the generation of form and space. The brilliant architect is as likely to be admired for his detailing as for his organisation of the plan or proportioning of an elevation.

An obvious way of overcoming this difficulty is to work with a structural and constructional system which has itself been explicitly defined. It is not surprising therefore that by far the largest and most comprehensive computer-aided architectural design packages have originated from large organisations committed to a particular system building technique. In the UK the HARNESS package for hospital design, the West Sussex County Architects system, the CEDAR 2 system of the Government Property Services Agency and the OXSYS system of the Oxford Regional Health Authority all rely heavily on the use of prescribed building components. These components are not only limited in number but also in jointing possibilities and in plan and section configuration. This has of course dramatically altered the nature of the design problem since the architect, whether he is aided by a computer or not, is now working within a closed universe of elements. Design has been reduced to a process of selection and disposition in which elements are selected from a catalogue. This is not the place for a critique of system building which, while it is clearly restrictive and limited in possibilities, has the potential to achieve economies of scale and standardisation. However it does seem that once the decision is taken to adopt system building computer-aided design seems increasingly attractive. The computer can be programmed with all the properties and dimensions of the components and the rules of assembly and consequently can assist not only with the selection of components but can also generate production drawings and other site assembly instructions.

Attempts have also been made to generate comprehensive computer-aided architectural design systems in which the user himself helps to generate and define the rules of the game. ARK-2, the pioneering system in the United States, allows the user to generate standard plan elements or deatil, which can then be recalled for incorporation into specific designs. The OXSYS system already mentioned is capable of using any constructional system which can be planned onto a rectangular tartan grid. The Scottish Special Housing Association package developed at Edinburgh University (Bijl 1972) allows the user to establish his own library of standard layouts and details, with the restriction of rectangular single and two-storey construction. There is, however, no evidence of architects generally adopting these semi-flexible packages. It is difficult at this stage to be sure just how much this is due to the restrictiveness of the systems or to the costs of running the large computer installations for which these packages were written.

An even more flexible approach to the problem of defining the rules of construction has been speculatively proposed by Frazer and Connor (1978). They suggest that the architect should be allowed to define an assembly of building components into a "key configuration". The nearest conventional concept to the key configuration is the structural bay but the authors prefer not to be restricted by the rectangular arrangement suggested by traditional techniques. This unit of structure forms the "seed" which the program is then able to "cultivate" by stretching, rotating and mutating to provide a range of elements capable of forming a complete building. Thus the designer working with such a system would be able to explore the architectural possibilities of a structural idea by injecting it into the computer and awaiting the outcome. It is of course by no means clear that such a technique, should it ever prove possible, would suit all designers. However it may well be attractive to those whose strategy is already focused upon the ordering of formal and practical constraints as seen for example in the writings of Bill Howell reported in chapter 11.

Implicit in Frazer and Connor's proposal is the notion that the computer may be able not just to play the role of calculator, scheduler and checker but also to explore, apparently creatively, possibilities not conceived of by the designer. Although this possibility was perceived by some workers very early in the life of computers comparatively little has yet been done to realise the potential, and indeed the opposite view of computers as restrictive and predictable still tends to hold sway. As long ago as 1950 Turing, one of the most influential early writers on artificial intelligence, refuted this restrictive view of computers. Byron's daughter is reported to have condemned Babbage's mechanical precursor of the electronic computer as having "no pretentions to originate anything". She maintained that such a device could only do as it was instructed. Now while this latter assertion is undoubtedly true, and even the modern computer is frequently described as a very high speed moron, it is grossly misleading. As Turing himself put it, this view of the computer assumes that "as soon as a fact is presented to a mind, all consequences of that fact spring into the mind simultaneously with it". Nothing of course could be further from the truth. As we have already observed, creativity remains one of the most intractable areas of psychology. No-one is able to guarantee that given a set of facts he will be able to deduce all the consequences and implications. The history of science alone must destroy such a naive belief. With the power and capacity of modern computers it is quite easy to write programs the precise outcome of which would be very difficult to predict.

Negroponte (1970) describes a robot which crawls around over maps reading them with photocells. GROPE, as it is called, is programmed to find "interesting things" and, for example may discover socio-economic patterns from geographically organised data. Another project at M.I.T. also described by Negroponte showed how a computer could be programmed to "learn" the visual mannerisms of designers and then use these implicit visual rules to generate solutions of its own. Practical applications of such ideas may well be some way off yet but they already suggest the potential of the computer as a possible aid to creativity which may well appeal to some, if not all, designers.

This role of the computer as a provoker and stimulator also frees us from the idea that the effects of a computer-aided design program are restricted to the particular project on which it may be used. Any

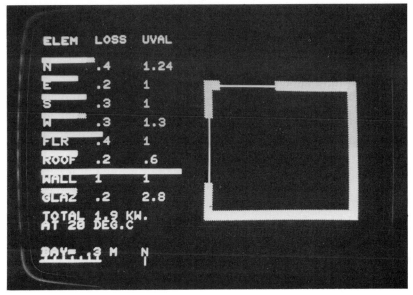

14.4(a)

computer program which in some way evaluates designs and outputs performance data may help the designer not just to develop a better solution to the specific problem in hand but also to learn how to produce better performing solutions in general. In fact it is also quite

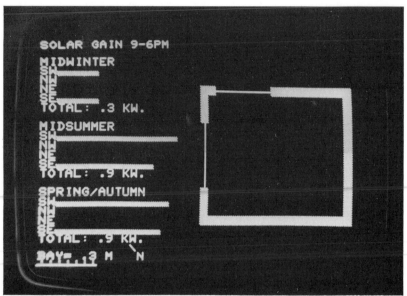

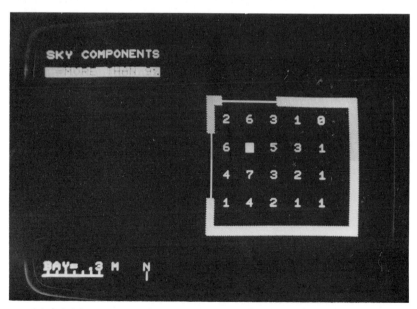

14.4(a),(b),(c) The ROOM program can show the heat loss, solar gain and daylighting performance of simple rooms

possible to use the computer in a purely educational role in design schools. For example the author has developed, with help from the Royal Institute of British Architects, a program intended to teach first year undergraduate architecture students how daylight, solar gain and heat loss interact in the design of windows. The student draws a room on the screen and inserts windows, and can discover the performance of his room in terms of its rates of heat loss and solar gain and in the distribution of daylight. Now the interaction between these three environmental factors is a complex one. The student however is able to develop an understanding of this interaction by changing the number, shape and position of windows, the orientation of the room, the size and shape of the room and the thermal properties of the building components. Such a program is thus not necessarily intended to be used on a particular design project but rather as a way of gaining experience quickly and easily.

As a teaching machine the computer offers many advantageous characteristics. It will respond rapidly and reliably. The calculations in the example just quoted take only seconds to perform even on the cheapest micro-processor but would take many hours by hand. Speedy "knowledge of results" has been shown to be a most important factor in learning. Imagine how difficult it would be to learn a golf swing if you only discovered where the ball landed several hours after hitting it! The computer will thus proceed at the pace of the operator, responding rapidly to his input and then waiting. A lecturer or teacher must inevitably proceed at what he judges to be the most suitable speed for the class as a whole, and can deliver the material in only one way. Interactive computer programs potentially allow the user to chart his own course through a problem. Thus a user of the room design program can isolate each of the variables in his own way. He is thus discovering about the problem for himself rather than being taught. When learning, we often make mistakes which while they seemed reasonable enough at the time, appeared foolish later. The fear of making such mistakes and appearing stupid often inhibits the learning process, and the computer, because of the very impersonal qualities which are so often criticised, can be helpful in this way too, allowing designers or students to try out ideas which may be ill-formed and half-baked but which may also contain some productive elements.

The educational role of the computer in design may be extended to involve others than just the designer. For example the ABACUS unit at Strathclyde University has been experimenting with a program called PARTIAL which allows the client to be directly involved with design

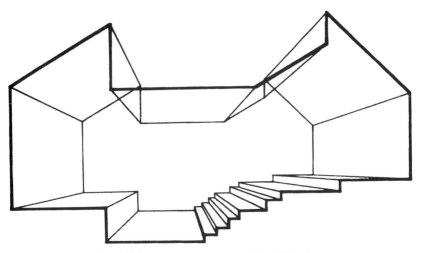

14.5 An example of high speed computer graphics. This drawing was produced from scratch in under a minute using the "gable 80" computer-aided architectural design package under development at Sheffield University

decision making. In these experiments (Aish 1977) nursery school headteachers who had no experience either of architectural design or computing used the program to design an eighty place nursery school. In this case the user was able to input and manipulate a plan while the computer would help by providing all the necessary draughting skill and by giving performance characteristics. These non-professional designers were thus able to discover for themselves the consequences of making all the various trade-offs possible in the scope of the problem. The trade-offs open to the user involved the number and area of the rooms within a given maximum building area, the degree of physical separation and enclosure of the various rooms and the external form of the building. As Aish puts it, the "participant can produce a graphically accurate drawing of his design idea (using computer graphics) while the calculative aspects of the program perform a value-free tutorial role and help him to bring his design within cost and performance limits". Unfortunately Aish does not publish any evaluation of the effectiveness of the program either in terms of the quality of building designed or terms of benefits to the users.

Regrettably this failure to appraise performance is all too often a characteristic of published work on computer-aided design, and writers such as Cross are justified in reminding us how much remains to be done before we are able to decide just how helpful computers can be to designers, and what roles they may play in the design process. It is important in this argument to be clear about the essential differences between human and machine intelligence. Although computers have been used to simulate human thought, the natural characteristics of people and machines are unmistakably distinct. These differences between the performance of man and machine were first highlighted by the American psychologist Paul Fitts, famous for his work on what he called "human performance theory" (Fitts 1951). The Fitts list as it became known shows how machines are characteristically accurate, consistent and precise compared to humans but also consequently inflexible, qualitative and tedious to program.

The designers of systems involving both men and machines have thus attempted to combine the attributes of men and machines to the best overall effect. Often such man-machine systems are required to make decisions in order to control some process or operation. The flight deck of a modern aircraft or the control room of a nuclear power station are both examples of the nerve centre of a system which can no more be fully automated than it could survive entirely without information processing machines. For their part the machines are rapid, precise, reliable and eternally vigilant, while the human ability to make balanced and integrated judgements when faced with unpredictable situations is undeniably vital.

Clearly designing is not amenable to techniques of total automation, although it is fair to point out that we have already learnt how to build and program machines with a much greater flexibility of response than was possible in Fitts' time. Nevertheless it may seem reasonable to view the design of a computer-aided design system as a man-machine decision making system analogous to process control problems of the type briefly discussed. Much has been written on the design of such systems and most authors in some way base their methodology on the Fitts list. Singleton (1974) for example shows a complete process in which the objectives of the system and thus its functions are first defined and then allocated to humans or machines on the basis of man-machine capabilities. The real difficulty with this approach towards computer-aided design is that we still understand so little of the process as practised by man that it is by no means easy to define the functions in the way that is intended by Singleton. As we saw in earlier chapters, design problems are rarely initially explicit, and thus even the designer himself is unsure of his goals. How then can we define goals except in a very general way before the designer even begins?

Whilst computer-aided design remains shrouded by so many unanswered questions there seems little doubt that work will continue. The existing research inertia and the promise of so many potential advantages of vastly increased information handling capacity are sufficient to motivate many to try to answer some of the questions. Whether the apparent advantages of computer-aided design will materialise or remain a mirage is as yet unclear. In the meantime men will continue to design by themselves, with others and, in a limited way, with computers. Sometimes their results will excite and inspire us but it is surely the design process itself which makes the most fascinating of studies. Perhaps we should hope never fully to understand the way designers think, for it is exactly because the designer does not know what he will think next which makes design such a challenging and satisfying occupation ...

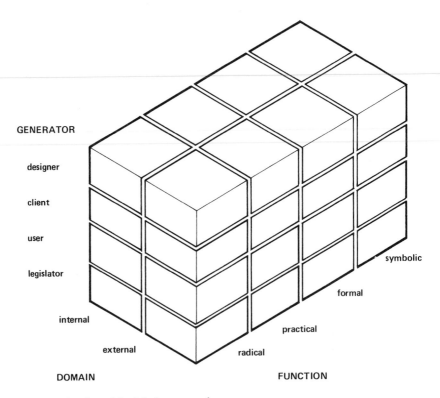

The completed model of design constraints.

BIBLIOGRAPHY

Aish, R. Prospects for design participation, *Design Methods and Theories*, vol 11 no 1, 1977

Alexander, C. Perception and modular co-ordination, *RIBA Journal*, London, October 1959

— *Notes on the Synthesis of Form*, McGraw Hill, New York, 1964

— A city is not a tree, *Design*, 206 pp 44–55, 1966

Archer, L. B. The structure of the design process, in Broadbent and Ward (eds), *Design Methods in Architecture*, Lund Humphries, London, 1969

Asimow, M. *Introduction to Design*, Prentice Hall, Englewood Cliffs, N. J., 1962

Bartlett, F. C. *Remembering*, Cambridge University Press, Cambridge, 1932

— *Thinking*, George Allen and Unwin, London, 1958

Baynes, K. *Attitudes in Design Education*, Lund Humphries, London, 1969

Bellini, M. The typewriter as 'just another limb', *Design*, 348, December 1977

Berlyne, D. E. *Structure and Direction in Thinking*, John Wiley, New York, 1965

Bijl, A. Application of CAAD research in practice: a system for house design, in *Proceedings of the International Conference on Computers in Architecture*, British Computer Society, 1972

Boje, A. *Open-plan Offices*, Business Books, 1971

Broadbent, G. *Design in Architecture*, John Wiley, New York, 1973

Buckle, R. *Modern Ballet Design*, Adam & Charles Black, London, 1955

Burton, R., Ahrends, P. and Koralek, P. Small group design and the idea of quality, *RIBA Journal*, vol 78, no 6, June 1971

Chermayeff, S. and Alexander, C. *Community and Privacy*,

Penguin, Harmondsworth, 1963

Chomsky, N. *Language and Mind*, Harcourt Brace and World, New York, 1968

Clegg, G. L. *The Design of Design*, Cambridge University Press, Cambridge 1969

Critchlow, K. *Order in Space: a design source book*, Thames and Hudson, London, 1969

Cross, N. (ed) *Design participation*, Academy Editions, London, 1972

— *Design and Technology*, The Open University Press, Milton Keynes, 1975

— *The Automated Architect*, Pion, 1977

— Design, research and society – some responses to Tom Maver, *Design Research* no 4, 1978

Cross, N. and Roy, R. *Design Methods Manual*, The Open University Press, Milton Keynes, 1975

Daley, J. A philosophical critique of behaviourism in architectural design, in Broadbent and Ward (eds) *Design Method in Architecture*, Lund Humphries, London, 1969

Darke, J. The primary generator and the design process, in W. E. Rogers and W. H. Ittelson (eds) *New Directions in Environmental Design Research*: proceedings of EDRA 9, pp 325–337, Washington EDRA, 1978

de Bono, E. *The Five Day Course in Thinking*, Allen Lane, Harmondsworth, 1968

— *Lateral Thinking: a text book of creativity*, Ward Lock Educational, London, 1970

— *Practical Thinking*, Jonathan Cape, London, 1971

— *Teaching Thinking*, Temple Smith, London, 1976

De Groot, A. D. *Thought and Choice in Chess*, Mouton, The Hague, 1965

Dickson, D. *Alternative Technology and the Politics of Technical Change*, Fontana, London, 1974

Eastman, C. M. On the analysis of intuitive design processes, in G. T. Moore (ed) *Emerging Methods in Environmental Design and Planning*, M.I.T. Press, Cambridge, Mass., 1970

Eberhard, J. P. We ought to know the difference, in G. T. Moore (ed) *Emerging Methods in Environmental Design and Planning*, M.I.T. Press, Cambridge, Mass., 1970

Elliot, P. *The Sociology of the Professions*, Macmillan, London, 1972

Evans, B. N., Powell, J. A. and Talbot, R. J. (eds) *Changing Design*, John Wiley, New York, 1980

Fitts, P. M. Engineering psychology and equipment design, in S. S. Stevens (ed) *Handbook of Experimental Psychology*, John Wiley, New York, 1951

Fitts, P. M. and Posner, M. *Human Performance*, Brooks/Cole, Monterey, California, 1967

Foster, N. Exploring the client's range of options. *RIBA Journal*, vol 77 no 6, June 1970

Frazer, J. H. and Connor, J. M. A conceptual seeding technique for architectural design, in *Proceedings of PARC 79* conference on computer aided architectural design On-line Conferences

Garner, W. R. *Uncertainty and Structure as Psychological Concepts*, John Wiley, New York, 1962

Getzels, J. W. and Jackson, P. W. *Creativity and Intelligence: Explorations with gifted children*, John Wiley, New York, 1962

Gordon, W. J. J. *Synectics: the Development of Creative Capacity*, Harper and Row, New York, 1961

Gosling, W. The relevance of system engineering in J. C. Jones and D. G. Thornley (eds) *Conference on Design Methods*, Pergamon, Oxford, 1963

Green, C. Learning to design, *Journal of Architectural Research and Teaching*, vol 2 no 1, 1971

— Design, games and language, *Build International*, vol 6 no 6, Nov 1973

— Gambit, *Faculty of Architectural Studies occasional paper* no A4, University of Sheffield, 1977

Green, P. *Design Education: problem solving and visual experience*, Batsford, London, 1974

Gregory, S. A. *The Design Method*, Butterworths, London, 1966

Gropius, W. *The New Architecture and the Bauhaus*, Faber and Faber, London, 1935

Guilford, J. P. The structure of intellect, *Psychological Bulletin*, no 53 p 267–293, 1956

— *The Nature of Human Intelligence*, McGraw Hill, New York, 1967

Habraken, N. J. *Supports: An alternative to mass housing*, The Architectural Press, London, 1972

Hackney, R. The architect as a community organiser, *RIBA Journal*, vol 84 no 7, July 1976

Handler, A. B. *Systems Approach to Architecture*, Elsevier, 1970

Hanson, K.   Design from linked requirements in a housing problem, in Broadbent and Ward *Design Methods in Architecture*, Lund Humphries, London, 1969

Hedge, A. and Lawson, B. R.   Creative thinking, in Singleton, W. T. (ed) *The Study of Real Skills, vol 2, Compliance and Excellence*, M.T.P. Press, Lancaster, 1980

Hertzberger, M.   Looking for the beach under the pavement, *RIBA Journal*, vol 78 no 8, August 1971

Hillier, B. and Leaman, A.   A new approach to architectural research, *RIBA Journal*, vol 79 no 12, December 1972

— How is design possible? *Journal of Architectural Research*, vol 3 no 1, 1974

Hillier, B., Musgrove, J. and O'Sullivan, P.   Knowledge and design, in W. J. Mitchell (ed) *Environmental Design: research and practice*, EDRA 3 – University of California, 1972

Honikman, B.   *AP 70: proceedings of the architectural psychology conference at Kingston Polytechnic*, RIBA Publications, London, 1971

Howell, W. G.   Vertebrate buildings: the architecture of structured space, *RIBA Journal*, vol 77 no 3, March 1970

Hudson, L.   *Contrary Imaginations: a psychological study of the English schoolboy*, Methuen, London, 1966

— *Frames of Mind: ability, perception and self-perception in the arts and sciences*, Methuen, London, 1968

Jenkins, J. G.   *The English Farm Wagon*, David and Charles, Newton Abbot, 1972

Jones, J. C.   Design methods reviewed, in S. A. Gregory (ed) *The Design Method*, 1966

Jones, J. C.   *Design methods: seeds of human futures*, John Wiley, New York, 1970

Jones, J. C. and Thornley, D. G.   *Conference on Design Methods*, Pergamon, Oxford, 1963

Kaye, B.   *The Development of the Architectural Profession in Britain: a sociological study*, Allen and Unwin, London, 1960

Kneller, G. F.   *The Art and Science of Creativity*, Holt, Rinehart and Winston, New York, 1965

Koestler, A.   *The Ghost in the Machine*, Hutchinson, London, 1967

Kuhn, T. S.   *The Structure of Scientific Revolutions*, University of Chicago Press, Chicago, 1962

Lacey, D.   An architect's approach to architecture, *RIBA Journal*, vol 72 no 6, June 1965

Lasdun, D. An architect's approach to architecture, *RIBA Journal*, vol 72 no 4, April 1965

— *A Language and a Theme*, RIBA Publications, London, 1976

Lawson, B. R. Open and closed ended problem solving in architectural design, in Honikman, B. (ed) *A. P. 70 proceedings of the architectural psychology conference at Kingston Polytechnic*, RIBA Publications, London 1971

— Problem solving in architectural design, PhD thesis University of Aston in Birmingham, 1972

— Upside down and back to front: architects and the building laws, *RIBA Journal*, vol 82 no 4, April 1975

— The architect as a designer, in W. T. Singleton (ed) *The Study of Real Skills, vol 1: The analysis of practical skills*, M.T.P. Press, Lancaster, 1978

— Computer potential in design education, *RIBA Journal*, vol 85 no 4, April 1978

— Cognitive strategies in architectural design, *Ergonomics*, vol 22 no 1, January 1979

— The act of designing, *Design Methods and Theories*, vol 13 no 1, Jan–April 1979

— Science, legislation and architecture, in B. N. Evans, J. A. Powell and R. J. Talbot (eds) *Changing Design*, John Wiley, New York, 1980

Lawson, B. R. and Spencer, C. P. Architectural intentions and user responses: the psychology building at Sheffield, *Architects' Journal*, vol 167 no 18, 1978

Laxton, M. Design education in practice, in K. Baynes (ed) 1969 *Attitudes in Design Education*, Lund Humphries, London, 1969

Leach, E. *A Runaway World?* the Reith Lectures 1967, BBC Publications, London, 1968

Le Corbusier *Towards a New Architecture*, The Architectural Press, London, 1946

— *The Modulor*, Faber and Faber, London, 1951

Levin, P. H. The design process in planning, *Town Planning Review*, vol 37 no 1, 1966

— Decision making in urban design, Building Research Station current paper, *Design* series no 49, 1966

Logcher, R. D., Flachsbart, B. B., Hall, E. J., Power, C. M. and Wells, R. A. *ICES STRUDL 1: Engineering User's Manual*, M.I.T. Press, Cambridge, Mass., 1967

Luchins, A. S. and Luchins, E. H. New experimental attempts at preventing mechanisation in problem solving, *Journal of General Psychology*, 42, 279–297, 1950

Lynn, J. Park Hill redevelopment, Sheffield, *RIBA Journal*, vol 69 no 12, December 1962

Lyons, E. Too often we justify our ineptitudes by moral postures, *RIBA Journal*, vol 75 no 5, May 1968

MacCormac, R. Design development: lightweight timber housing, *Architects' Journal*, 26 Nov 1975

Mackinnon, D. W. The nature and nurture of creative talent, *Walter Van Dyke Bingham Lecture*, Yale University, 11 April 1962

— The assessment and development of managerial creativity, *Creativity Network*, vol 2 no 3, 1976

McLuhan, M. *The Medium is the Message*, Penguin, Harmondsworth, 1967

Maguire, R. Nearness to need, *RIBA Journal*, vol 78 no 4, April 1971

Maier, N. R. F. Reasoning in humans: the solution of a problem and its appearance in consciousness, *Journal of Comparative Psychology*, 12, 181–194, 1931

March L. and Steadman, P. *The Geometry of Environment*, Methuen, London, 1974

Markus, T. A. The role of building performance measurement and appraisal in design method, in G. Broadbent and A. Ward (eds) *Design Methods in Architecture*, Lund Humphries, London, 1969

— Design and research, *Conrad*, vol 1 no 2, July 1969

— A doughnut model of the environment and its design in N. Cross (ed) *Design Participation*, Academy Editions, London 1972

Matchett, E. Control of thought in creative work, *Chartered Mechanical Engineer*, vol 14 no 4, 1968

Maver, T. W. Appraisal in the building design process, in G. T. Moore (ed) *Emerging Methods in Environmental Design and Planning*, M.I.T. Press, Cambridge, Mass., 1970

Meadow, A. and Parnes, S. J. Evaluation of training in creative problem solving, *Journal of Applied Psychology*, 43, 3, 1959

Miller, G. A., Galanter, E., and Pribram, K. H. *Plans and the Structure of Behaviour*, Holt Rinehart and Winston, New York, 1960

Mitchell, W. J. Experiments with participation oriented computer systems, in N. Cross (ed) *Design Participation*, Academy Editions, London, 1972

— *Computer-Aided Architectural Design*, Petrocelli-Charter,

Princeton, New Jersey, 1977

Moore, G. T. (ed) *Emerging Methods in Environmental Design and Planning*, M.I.T. Press, Cambridge, Mass., 1970

Mueller, R. E. *The Science of Art (the cybernetics of creative communication)*, Rapp and Whiting, London, 1967

Murphy, G. *Personality: a biosocial approach to origins and structure*, Harper & Row, New York, 1947

Negroponte, N. *The Architecture Machine*, M.I.T. Press, Cambridge, Mass., 1970

— *Soft Architecture Machines*, M.I.T. Press, Cambridge, Mass., 1975

Neisser, U. *Cognitive Pyschology*, Appleton Century Crofts, New York, 1967

Newell, A., Simon, H. A. and Shaw, J. C. Elements of a theory of human problem solving, *Psychological Review*, vol 65 no 3, 1958

Norburg-Schultz, C. *Meaning in Western Architecture*, Studio Vista, London, 1975

Opron, R. The Renault method, *Design*, 333, September 1976

Osborn, A. F. *Applied Imagination* (3rd Ed), Charles Scribner, New York, 1957

Osgood, C. E. The nature and measurement of meaning, *Psychological Bulletin*, vol 49 no 3, 1952

Page, J. K. Review of the papers presented at the conference, in J. C. Jones and D. Thornley (eds) *Conference on Design Methods*, Pergamon, Oxford, 1963

— in *Building for people*, 1965 conference report, Ministry of Public Building and Works, London, 1966

— Planning and protest, in N. Cross (ed) *Design Participation*, Academy Editions, London, 1972

Poincaré, H. Mathematical creation, in P. E. Vernon (ed) *Creativity*, Penguin, London, 1924

Price, C. Anticipatory design, *RIBA Journal*, vol 84 no 7, July 1976

Pugin, A. W. N. *The True Principles of Pointed or Christian Architecture*, London, 1841

Rae, J. Games, *Architects' Journal*, vol 15 no 149, 1969

Rand, P. *Thoughts on Design*, Studio Vista, London, 1970

Rapoport, A. *Fights, Games and Debates*, University of Michigan Press, Ann Arbor, 1960

RIBA *Architectural Practice and Management Handbook*, RIBA Publications, London, 1965

Rittel, H. W. J. and Webber, M. M. Dilemmas in a general theory of planning, *Policy Sciences*, 4 1973

Roberts, J. M., Arth, M. J., Bush, R. R. Games in culture, *American Anthropologist* no 61, 1959

Roe, A. A psychologist examines sixty-four eminent scientists, *Scientific American*, vol 187, pp 21–25, 1952

Rosenstein, A. B., Rathbone, R. R. and Schneerer, W. F. *Engineering Communications*, Prentice Hall, Englewood Cliffs, New Jersey, 1964

Ryle, G. *The Concept of Mind*, Hutchinson, London, 1949

Savidge, R. Revise the regs: the plan revealed, *Architects' Journal*, vol 167 no 14, 1978

Simon, H. A. *The Sciences of the Artificial*, M.I.T. Press, Cambridge, Mass., 1969

Singleton, W. T. *Man-Machine Systems*, Penguin, Harmondsworth, 1974

— (ed) *The Study of Real Skills*, vol 1, *The analysis of practical skills*, M.T.P. Press, 1978

— (ed) *The Study of Real Skills, vol 2, Compliance and excellence*, M.T.P. Press, 1980

Smith, I. Architects approach to architecture, *RIBA Journal*, vol 74 no 7, July 1967

Smith, P. F. *The Dynamics of Urbanism*, Hutchinson Educational, London, 1974

Stevens, S. S. (ed) *Handbook of Experimental Psychology*, John Wiley, New York, 1951

Stirling, J. An architect's approach to architecture, *RIBA Journal*, vol 72 no 5, May 1965

Sturt, G. *The Wheelwright's Shop*, Cambridge University Press, Cambridge, 1923

Toffler, A. *Futureshock*, Bodley Head, London, 1970

Turing, A. M. Computing machinery and intelligence, *Mind*, vol 59, pp 433–450, 1950

Utzon, J. Account of the Sydney Opera House, *Architecture in Australia*, Dec 1965

Von Neumann, J. and Morgenstern, O. *Theory of Games and Economic Behaviour*, Princeton University Press, Princeton, New Jersey, 1949

Watkin, D. *Morality and Architecture*, Clarendon Press, Oxford, 1977

Watson, J. D. *The Double Helix: a personal account of the discovery of the structure of DNA*, Weidenfeld and Nicolson, London, 1968

Wehrli, R.   Open-ended problem solving in design, PhD Thesis, University of Utah, 1968

Weinberg, A. M.   Can technology replace social engineering? reprinted in N. Cross, D. Elliott, R. Roy (eds) *Man Made Futures*, Hutchinson Educational/Open University, London, 1974

Wertheimer, M.   *Productive Thinking* (enlarged edition), Harper & Row, New York, 1959

Whitfield, P. R.   *Creativity in Industry*, Penguin, Harmondsworth, 1975

Wittgenstein, L.   *Philosophical Investigations*, Basil Blackwell, Oxford, 1967

Woodford, G., Williams, K. and Hill, N.   *The Value of Standards for the External Residential Environment*, Department of the Environment research report 6, London, 1976

Index